THE GATHERED TABLE

A Taste of Home

COMPILED BY GATHER & GATHER IRELAND
IN AID OF
PETER McVERRY TRUST

NINE BEAN ROWS

Contents

Foreword

Home means something special to many of us. It's a place for family, home cooking, laughter and rest. It's our sanctuary. And for those who have lived without a home, it means everything.

For the people we work with in Peter McVerry Trust, home means safety, security and independence. It's the simple joy of coming and going as you please or sharing a meal with a loved one. It can be a place to restart their lives or to reunite their families.

Peter McVerry Trust is a national housing and homelessness charity that is committed to reducing homelessness. Our charity was founded in 1983 by Fr Peter McVerry to provide housing and support for young people experiencing homelessness. Since then, we have progressed from providing a three-bedroom flat in Ballymun to today's wide range of services catering for the diverse needs of people impacted by homelessness.

A decade ago homelessness felt like a big-city problem, but today it touches every county in Ireland. In 2022, Peter McVerry Trust helped over 10,000 people in towns and cities all across the country.

This year we mark our fortieth anniversary. While the charity has grown significantly, our ethos and vision have remained the same: an Ireland that supports all those on the margins and upholds their rights to full inclusion in society. Our services are based on the principles of respect, choice and dignity.

Peter McVerry Trust works to support people in homelessness and also to prevent people who are at risk of homelessness ever entering homeless services. We have a number of services to support this work, including emergency homeless accommodation for individuals and families, Learning Centres, addiction and recovery services, housing supports, U18s and Aftercare accommodation and our Housing First programme.

Housing First is a vital piece of the puzzle in reducing the number of people in homelessness across Ireland. The Housing First model provides a person sleeping rough with their own secure accommodation as well as access to intensive and specialised support services.

As an early adopter and major supporter of Housing First, Peter McVerry Trust has been working on the model since 2011. Today, over 80% of our Housing First participants retain their homes and their tenancies. In the coming years, we plan to grow this programme and give more people the key to their own front door – and the support they need to maintain their new home.

The ethos behind Housing First is the same as our founder's: the solution to homelessness is to give people a home. Yet securing homes for social

Home means something special to many of us. It's a place for family, home cooking, laughter and rest. It's our sanctuary. And for those who have lived without a home, it means everything.

Each story has a common thread: the life-changing impact of having a home of your own.

housing is becoming more and more difficult. The supply of homes is limited and private rents are increasing.

Over the past 40 years, we have focused our resources on increasing our own housing stock to provide direct access to housing for people living in homelessness. As a specialist approved housing body, Peter McVerry Trust is a key provider of social housing for people exiting homelessness and those at risk of homelessness, such as care leavers.

In 2004 our resources allowed us to purchase our first two apartment units for housing. At the end of 2022, Peter McVerry Trust will deliver its one thousandth unit.

Peter McVerry Trust is one of Ireland's leading advocates for action on empty homes, derelict sites and underused spaces. Addressing these issues can play a significant role in improving housing availability and housing affordability as well as reducing and ultimately eliminating homelessness.

Our housing development work demonstrates how empty homes can be reused to provide high-quality social housing. Today, 85% of our housing pipeline is generated from empty or derelict homes projects.

These projects work on many levels. The buildings are an undesirable purchase for many so we're not in direct competition with first-time buyers. They're derelict and an eyesore, so converting them into homes revitalises town centres and reduces anti-social behaviour. It's a key focus for our

organisation in the coming years and will allow us to give more people the key to their own front door.

All this work would not be possible without the people who support our charity. Our loyal corporate partners and generous donors are crucial to our charity and enable us to continue our work and help more people impacted by homelessness.

Since I joined Peter McVerry Trust as its first CEO in 2005, I've had the privilege of hearing thousands of success stories from the people we have supported. Each story has a common thread: the life-changing impact of having a home of your own.

Throughout this book, you will hear from some of the people we have supported out of homelessness. They have shared what their new home means to them and how it has changed their lives.

I would like to thank Gather & Gather and all their fantastic partners who brought this book to life. The world needs more people who share their gifts to help those who need it the most.

I also want to thank you for buying this book and helping us to give more people a home of their own. Your contribution will enable us to change more lives. I hope that these recipes bring joy to you and your loved ones.

Pat Doyle
CEO, Peter McVerry Trust

Introduction

At Gather & Gather, food is our world – it has the power to inspire and connect us all.

The Gather & Gather ethos is all about using great food to bring people together to enjoy good conversation and company, whatever the occasion, the location or the time of day. We love big-flavoured, unpretentious cooking using local ingredients that are cooked with care and made into something delicious to eat.

Mark Anderson, our culinary director, brought me the idea of creating a cookbook back in 2021. We had been involved with the Peter McVerry Trust for several years. Fundraising is always a challenge and we had been looking for a project that would make an impact in supporting their work. Given Ireland's current level of homelessness, it's a critical need.

As a team, we know food and hospitality; it's what we do best. This idea of bringing together a collection of cherished recipes from cooks across all sectors of Ireland's food industry – from bakers and butchers, farmers and food champions to producers, shopkeepers and chefs – made sense.

We invited the contributors to send us their favourite recipe to cook at home, the one that takes them back to happy times: Sunday lunches with all the family, summer barbecues with laughter in the air, dinners spent with friends sitting around the table chatting about everything and nothing, a glass of your favourite wine in hand.

Food is intrinsically tied to some of our fondest memories, those special occasions that prompt family get-togethers. We wanted this cookbook to both celebrate memories around food (and perhaps create new ones) and to emphasise the importance of a safe home. Across the country, millions of us take it for granted that we finish the day by enjoying a meal in the sanctuary of our home, often in the company of family or friends as part of that daily ritual. But this is only the reality for some.

Having a place to call home is precious. All of us will have felt the strain of staying in our homes during the pandemic, but the pandemic has been even more frightening for those without a place to call home. Through its services, the Peter McVerry Trust has created pathways out of homelessness and into a secure environment. They have worked tirelessly on the frontline, looking after the most vulnerable and marginalised in society.

A cookbook's role in raising awareness of homelessness may not be apparent at first glance, but it becomes more evident when you consider the relationship between our food and our security and comfort.

For me, a good cookbook does so much more than teach me how to cook a dish. Great cookbooks carry real meaning, reflecting memories of people or places. They also present future aspirations to those who read and use them. Many of the things we cook have a story: a past, present and future. But behind all that, a cookbook is also a collection of cherished recipes that best represent the contributors' love of food, gathered together to share.

The Gathered Table: A Taste of Home is a celebration of that beautiful, comforting spirit. Every time you use this extraordinary book, I hope you are reminded of that spirit, exemplified in Peter McVerry Trust's ongoing work helping homeless people to find a home for good.

Pauline Cox
Managing Director, Gather & Gather Ireland

GATHER
— & —
GATHER

'A cookbook's role in raising awareness of homelessness may not be apparent at first glance, but it becomes more evident when you consider the relationship between our **food** and our **security** and **comfort**.'

Pauline Cox, Gather & Gather Ireland

Bread & Breakfast

Porridge bread

Aisling and Michael Flanagan, Velvet Cloud

Porridge bread is one of the most popular recipes on our website. It can be added to and adapted according to your taste – it's hard to get it wrong. Some people like to sweeten it with dried fruit and honey, while others like to swap out some of the oats for spelt or wholemeal flour. A gluten-free version can also be made using gluten-free oats and bread soda.

At home on the farm, we like to keep it simple. We find it's a great way of getting the goodness of porridge and yogurt into the junior shepherds. They wolf it down while it's still warm, straight out of the oven, or toasted with lots of butter.

Makes 1 loaf

butter or oil, for greasing

450g Velvet Cloud sheep's yogurt

1 egg, beaten

300g porridge oats, plus extra for sprinkling

2 tsp baking soda

2 tbsp mixed seeds (optional)

½ tsp salt (optional)

Preheat the oven to 180°C (160°C fan). Grease a 900g (2lb) loaf tin or line with non-stick baking paper.

Put the yogurt and beaten egg in a large bowl and stir well.

Mix the oats and baking soda with the seeds and salt (if using) in a separate bowl, then add this to the yogurt mixture and stir thoroughly. Scrape into the greased or lined loaf tin and sprinkle a little extra oats on top.

Bake in the preheated oven for 30 minutes, then lower the temperature to 150°C (130°C fan) and cook for a further 30 minutes. Cool on a wire rack.

{tip}
You can also make this bread using Velvet Cloud yogurt that you have frozen and then defrosted.

Buttermilk batch bread

Eoin Cluskey, Bread 41

As someone who spent years travelling away from home, for me the idea of home has always transcended a physical place. A home is about togetherness, and it's food that brings us together. If you think about some of your most cherished memories, many of them likely involve food. Whether it's sitting around a table having dinner or catching up with friends over a coffee and croissant, food is the centre of every home.

For far too long, bread has been seen as something that you just put stuff on to make it taste good, as a vessel to carry something. But it is food in and of itself. It has flavour and it can deliver so much while asking for so little. This recipe is special because I love making bread. My grandmother taught me how to make my very first loaf and real bread has been my driving passion ever since. It's why I got into this industry: to make bread and to get more people eating real bread.

Makes 4 small loaves

575g strong white flour

12g salt

12g fresh yeast

400g buttermilk

oil, for greasing

Mix the flour and salt in a large bowl. Crumble the yeast into the flour, then add the buttermilk.

Bring the dough together with your hands or a spatula. Turn the dough out on a clean surface and knead for about 10 minutes. The dough should be soft and elastic.

Place the dough in an oiled bowl, cover with a clean damp tea towel and leave to prove for around 1½ hours. The proving time depends on the temperature of your kitchen, so the most important thing is that dough has doubled in size. It will be active, fluffy and have expanded significantly.

Turn the proved dough out onto the countertop and knock it back. Divide the dough into four equal portions (about 250g each). Shape each portion of dough into a rough round and leave them to rest.

Once the dough has rested, roll each portion into a tight round and place on a baking tray in a 2 x 2 pattern, allowing each portion of dough to just touch each other. Cover and allow to prove again for 60–90 minutes, until well risen.

Preheat the oven to 220°C (200°C fan). Put a roasting tray in the base of the oven.

Put the loaves in the hot oven, then pour water from a boiling kettle into the hot roasting tray to create a blast of steam. Bake for 35–40 minutes, until the base sounds hollow when tapped. Cool on a wire rack.

Soda bread

Michelle Darmody, activist, researcher and food writer

The smell of a loaf of soda bread baking in the oven evokes home for me. I love cutting off a slice, still warm, and covering it in butter and marmalade. This native Irish bread is simple yet versatile. A slice can be served with a comforting bowl of soup, alongside a salad or turned into a cheesy melt.

Makes 1 loaf

250g whole wheat flour

180g plain flour

20g porridge oats,
plus an extra handful

1 tbsp mixed seeds

1 tsp baking soda

1 tsp salt

350ml buttermilk

1 egg, lightly beaten

2 tsp honey

Preheat the oven to 240°C (220°C fan). Oil a 900g (2lb) loaf tin. Cut a long strip of parchment paper that lines the base of the tin and comes up along the narrow ends of the tin and over the edges. This long piece of parchment will help you ease the warm loaf out of the tin by pulling each end of the strip. Alternatively, you can form the loaf into the traditional round shape on a baking tray lined with non-stick baking paper.

Mix the flours, porridge oats and seeds together in a large bowl. Sieve in the baking soda and salt, then stir them in well.

Mix the buttermilk, egg and honey together in a jug. Make a well in the dry ingredients and stir in the wet.

Scrape the mixture into the prepared tin. Sprinkle some porridge oats on top and press a knife along the centre to make a slit in the loaf. Alternatively, form the dough into a round, put it on the lined tray and cut a deep cross on the top, then sprinkle some porridge oats on top.

Bake in the preheated oven for 10 minutes, then reduce the oven temperature to 210°C (190°C fan) and bake for a further 40 minutes, until the bread is golden on top and a skewer inserted into the centre of the loaf comes out clean.

If using the tin, use the ends of the baking parchment to help you ease the loaf from the tin. Allow to cool on a wire rack.

Banana bread

Ellie Kisyombe, Eillie's Kitchen Home Edition

It has become difficult to keep up with what we used to call normal life. We are living in uncertain times, afraid of what is going to happen next. But here is a simple recipe that you can make from ingredients you may already have at home. Bananas can turn over-ripe quickly, but there's no need to throw them in the bin – use them to make this banana bread for the family to have with tea.

Makes 1 loaf

4 over-ripe bananas

50g butter or coconut oil, softened

100g brown sugar

2 eggs

50ml natural yogurt

240g plain flour

2 tsp baking powder

juice of ½ orange or lemon

30g coconut flakes or desiccated coconut

For the orange and cinnamon coulis:

170g brown sugar

250ml water

1 cinnamon stick

1 tsp mixed spice

1 orange, thinly sliced

Preheat the oven to 200°C (180°C fan). Grease a 900g (2lb) loaf tin or line it with non-stick baking paper.

Peel your bananas and put them into a blender, then blitz until they are a smooth purée.

Put the butter or coconut oil and the brown sugar in a large bowl and cream together until well incorporated. Beat in the eggs one at a time, then stir in the yogurt.

Add the flour and the baking powder and mix until just combined, then add the banana purée and the orange or lemon juice, mixing well. Lastly, add the coconut.

Pour the batter into the prepared baking tin. Bake in the preheated oven for about 50 minutes, until a skewer inserted into the centre comes out clean.

To make the coulis, put all the ingredients in a small saucepan and bring to a boil, then reduce the heat and let it simmer until it reduces down to a nice thick syrup. Allow to cool slightly.

Once your cake is done, brush it all over with the cooled coulis. You can put the orange slices on top of your cake to make it look more colourful and put the cinnamon stick on top too if you like. Allow to cool on a wire rack, then cut into slices to serve.

Coconut, honey and vanilla granola

Ruth Hegarty, egg&chicken consulting

This granola recipe takes only minutes to make – no weighing of ingredients required, just use any size cup you like to measure them. It stays fresh and crunchy for ages once it's kept in an airtight container, so you can make it in bulk and have an instant, but gourmet, breakfast or snack. I love it with natural yogurt and stewed rhubarb or fresh raspberries when we have them in the garden. It also makes a nice gift – reuse some large glass jars to give some to friends. I include a jar as part of the homemade food gifts I give every Christmas and it always goes down well.

Makes 1 large jar

5 cups porridge or jumbo oats
(Kilbeggan organic oats have
outstanding flavour)

1 cup desiccated coconut

½ cup dark brown sugar

½ cup sunflower seeds

½ cup pumpkin seeds

½ cup sunflower oil

½ cup honey

2 tsp vanilla extract

Preheat the oven to 200°C. If you have a smaller top oven, use that to save energy. A fan oven is not needed for this, as you will be stirring the granola at intervals during cooking.

Put a large piece of non-stick baking paper in a roasting tin so that it comes up around the edges. Just pop it in loosely – it prevents the granola from sticking to the tin and makes it easier to stir.

Put the oats in the tin, making sure there is enough space to stir in the other ingredients later on. Bake the oats on their own in the preheated oven for 10 minutes, then remove the tin from the oven and stir in the coconut, brown sugar and seeds.

Add the oil, honey and vanilla and mix them through thoroughly to coat the oats and seeds as evenly as possible. You can do this with a large spoon but it's more effective to use your hands.

Return the tin to the oven and bake for a total of 20 minutes more, taking the tin out every 5 minutes to stir. The oats on the top and at the edges will brown more quickly, so stirring is key.

Remove the tin from the oven and allow the granola to cool on the parchment, using your hands or a spoon to break it up as it cools. When it's completely cool, store the granola in an airtight container.

Fried eggs
with pickled red onions, dukkah, harissa yogurt and paprika butter

Keith Coleman, private chef

This dish was first manifested on my days off from running a busy café in Dublin. Tired, under-caffeinated and not exactly in the mood for cooking a fry, it pulls together a lot of what you may have in the pantry already. It works perfectly for breakfast or brunch and I have even been known to serve it for 'brinner'. It also works well for serving multiple brunch guests, as you can make all the elements in advance and then it's just a matter of frying some eggs. You can plate this up individually or let everyone figure it out for themselves.

Serves 6

For the pickled red onions:

500g red onions, very thinly sliced

10g fine sea salt

250ml lemon juice

For the dukkah:

500g skinless hazelnuts

150g sunflower seeds

150g sesame seeds

25g fennel seeds

25g cumin seeds

25g coriander seeds

25g nigella seeds

25g black peppercorns

15g paprika

20g flaky sea salt

For the harissa yogurt:

500g thick Greek yogurt

50g harissa paste

zest and juice of 1 lemon

To make the pickled pink onions, put the onions in a large bowl. Sprinkle over the salt, then massage it into the onions and allow to pickle for at least 30 minutes, until the salt has drawn liquid from the onions. Transfer the onions and their liquid to a large sterilised jar, then pour in just enough lemon juice to cover the onions, making sure they're submerged. Seal the jar and store in the fridge for up to two weeks.

To make the dukkah, preheat the oven to 180°C (160°C fan). Spread the hazelnuts and sunflower seeds on separate baking trays and toast in the preheated oven for about 15 minutes, until golden brown. Allow to cool.

Meanwhile, toast the sesame seeds in a dry heavy-based pan over a low heat until fragrant, then tip out onto a plate to cool. Put the fennel, cumin, coriander and nigella seeds, the black peppercorns and the paprika in the pan and toast just until they're fragrant too, then tip them out into the sesame seeds and allow everything to cool.

Put the cooled seeds and spices in a spice grinder or high-speed blender and blitz to a fine powder, then scrape out into a large bowl. Put the hazelnuts in a food processor and pulse until finely chopped, then scrape them into the bowl with the spice powder. Stir in the salt with a wooden spoon to bring it all together. Pour into a clean, dry jar – this will easily last for up to a month.

To make the harissa yogurt, mix the yogurt and half of the harissa paste together in a bowl. You start off with half the amount so that

For the paprika butter:

250g good-quality salted butter

25g red chilli flakes

25g smoked paprika

To finish:

1 loaf of good-quality bread

olive oil, for frying

eggs (1 or 2 per person)

feta cheese

fresh herbs (I like fennel fronds, lovage, mint and coriander, but use whatever you have)

you can taste it and then add more if you like. Stir in the lemon zest and juice, then set aside in the fridge until needed.

To make the paprika butter, put the butter, chilli flakes and smoked paprika in a high-sided saucepan and warm gently over a low heat for about 10 minutes, stirring often to make sure the paprika doesn't stick to the bottom of the pan and burn. Set aside and keep warm so that the butter remains melted.

To bring it all together, slice two thick pieces of bread per person. Toast it, but make sure it's not too crunchy.

Put a non-stick frying pan over a high heat and add a decent amount of olive oil, more than you'd normally use. The extra oil encourages your fried eggs to have crispy edges, which is crucial to the enjoyment of this dish. Crack the eggs into the hot oil, season each one with a little flaky salt and cook to your liking.

Meanwhile, spread some harissa yogurt on each plate. Once the eggs are fried, slide them onto the yogurt. Drizzle 1 tablespoon of paprika butter over the eggs, allowing it to pool into all the lovely crevices. Next up is the feta cheese, but go easy here as feta can be very salty. Sprinkle over some dukkah, scatter some slices of pickled onion over the eggs and finish the entire ensemble with some freshly picked herbs. I find the best way to enjoy this is to replace the knife in your hand with a piece of bread, using a fork to scoop whatever you fancy onto the bread.

{*tip*}

This would easily serve six people and even a couple kids. The quantities given for the different elements of the dish are large so that you have some left over for other nice things. Oftentimes you spend a lot of time cooking a recipe and have nothing left afterwards — you've got to factor in leftovers!

'I was the last person anyone expected could turn a house into a **home**, but I did with the right **support**. I have an amazing key worker from Peter McVerry Trust. Home means a lot to me. It means **safety** and **warmth**. Things are especially difficult for people with the cost of living now, but because I have a home, I feel **secure**. What was once an empty shell, just a house, is now my home. It completes a part of me. I'm blessed. Home means **independence** and **gratitude**.'

Ann-Marie, Louth

Beef

Irish beef cheek lasagne

Pat Whelan, James Whelan Butchers

This was one of our great discoveries when I was testing recipes for my book, *The Irish Beef Book* (Gill & Macmillan, 2013). It elevates the humble lasagne to another level entirely. The quantities given here for the ragù make enough for the lasagne, but I highly recommend that you double them and save the rest for another night – it actually gets better after sitting overnight in the fridge.

Serves 6–8

For the beef cheek ragù:

900g beef cheeks, trimmed

salt and freshly ground black pepper

1 tbsp extra virgin olive oil or Irish rapeseed oil, plus extra for greasing

60g smoked bacon, chopped into cubes

2 carrots, chopped

2 onions, chopped

2 celery sticks, chopped

2 x 400g tins of chopped tomatoes

200ml red wine

500ml chicken stock

2 sprigs of fresh thyme

1 tbsp aged balsamic vinegar

For the béchamel sauce:

70g butter

40g plain flour

1 litre milk

1 tsp salt

1 tsp freshly grated nutmeg

Preheat the oven to 170°C (150°C fan).

First make the ragù. Cut the beef cheeks in half and season with salt and pepper. Heat the oil in a heavy-based frying pan and fry the beef cheeks in batches, allowing them to brown and caramelise. Do not overcrowd the pan or the meat will steam rather than brown.

Meanwhile, in a large heavy-based casserole, fry the bacon until golden, then add the chopped vegetables and fry until softened. Add the tomatoes, then the browned beef cheeks.

Pour the red wine into the frying pan and scrape up any crispy bits, then add everything to the casserole. Add the chicken stock and thyme sprigs, cover and cook in the preheated oven for about 3 hours, by which time the beef cheeks should be falling apart.

Remove the lid and cook for a further 45 minutes, stirring occasionally, until some of the liquid has evaporated and you have a rich, thick sauce. Break up the meat with a wooden spoon. When the sauce has cooled slightly, add the vinegar, which adds richness, and check the seasoning. This ragù will be even better if you allow it to cool, refrigerate it overnight and use it the following day.

Preheat the oven to 200°C (180°C fan). >>

To assemble:

250g fresh lasagne sheets

100g finely grated hard cheese, e.g. Parmesan or an Irish cheese such as Coolea, Cratloe Hills, Desmond or Hegarty's Cheddar

To make the béchamel sauce, melt the butter in a medium saucepan over a low heat. Add the flour and stir until smooth. Cook for 6–7 minutes over a medium heat.

Meanwhile, heat the milk in a separate large saucepan until it's just about to boil. Gradually add the hot milk to the butter and flour mixture, whisking continuously until very smooth. Bring to a boil, then reduce the heat and cook for 10 minutes, stirring constantly. Remove the pan from the heat, season with the salt and nutmeg and set aside until ready to use.

Brush the bottom and sides of a lasagne dish with oil. Lay a couple fresh lasagne sheets on the bottom of the dish. Spread a layer of the meat sauce over the pasta, then pour on a layer of béchamel sauce. Sprinkle with a little finely grated cheese. Repeat the layers, ending with a pasta layer over which you spread the remaining béchamel and a final sprinkling of cheese.

Bake in the preheated oven for about 45 minutes, until heated through and nicely browned on top.

'It's now almost a year since I got my **home** and my partner moved in with me in February. I'm a lot more **independent**. You can't progress your life unless you have a base. You can't go to college or to work. It's somewhere to come home to make your **dinner** – we both like to cook. It's somewhere to feel safe. Somewhere to close off from the world. You **appreciate** the simple things. Peace and quiet, **rest**. I've been able to build my **confidence** and turn my life around here. For a long time, we didn't feel **safe**. But now we do. That's a basic human right.'

Niki, Cork

Mexican beef caldillo

Lily Ramirez-Foran, Picado

When I think of home, I always go to this broth. When the smells fill my kitchen, I'm transported back to my mother's noisy table in Mexico. It is my ultimate comfort food. I know the addition of banana might sound a bit weird, but don't knock it till you try it – the sweet and salty combination is truly delicious.

Serves 4–6

For the meat broth:

1kg beef skirt

½ head of garlic, unpeeled and left whole

1 tbsp salt

3 litres water

For the tomato sauce:

350g ripe tomatoes

1 garlic clove, peeled

1 tsp salt

½ tsp black peppercorns

1 tbsp olive oil

100g finely diced onion

65g finely diced red pepper

1 jalapeño chilli, left whole

1½ tbsp masa harina or cornflour

1 small bunch of fresh coriander (stalks and leaves), chopped

To serve:

2 underripe bananas, cut into thin slices

¼ onion, thinly sliced

fresh coriander leaves

corn tortillas, warmed

To make the broth, put the beef, garlic, salt and water in a large, heavy-based pot over a high heat. Bring to a boil, then reduce the heat to medium-low, cover with a lid and simmer for 1½–2 hours, until the meat is tender and just falling apart.

While the meat cooks, put the tomatoes, garlic, salt and peppercorns in a blender or food processor and blitz until smooth. Set aside. If you want, add a small amount of water (2 tablespoons maximum) to aid the blending process.

Heat the oil in a non-stick frying pan over a medium heat. Add the onion, red pepper and whole chilli. Gently fry just until the onion and pepper have softened.

Pour in the tomato sauce. Cook over a medium heat for 8–10 minutes, until everything is well cooked and the tomatoes have turned a wonderful deep red colour. Set aside until the broth is ready.

When the beef is done, take the chunks of meat out of the pot. Fish out and discard the garlic, then using two forks, shred the meat roughly.

Put 5 tablespoons of the warm beef broth in a cup with the masa harina or cornflour and mix into a paste until you get the consistency of Irish pancake batter. Set aside.

Pour the tomato sauce into the beef stock and mix well. Add the shredded beef to the soup and gently simmer over a medium heat for 5 minutes.

Reserve some of the coriander leaves for garnish, then chop the rest, stalks and all, and add to the soup along with the masa harina or cornflour paste. Stir to combine and check the seasoning. Reduce the heat to low and simmer for a further 10 minutes.

Serve hot with banana slices, thinly sliced raw onion, fresh coriander leaves and warm corn tortillas for a comforting meal.

Beef and red wine stew

Anna Haugh, Myrtle

When I was a kid we always made this like a traditional Irish stew, but when I grew up I discovered the delight of adding red wine. It makes it into a completely different dish.

Serves 4

olive oil

400g diced stewing beef

salt and freshly ground black pepper

100g rashers, chopped

1 onion, diced

4 garlic cloves, chopped

1 cinnamon stick

400ml red wine

600ml–1 litre chicken stock

3 carrots, diced

3 spring onions, thinly sliced at an angle

2 handfuls of chopped kale

a few cubes of butter

To serve:

mashed potatoes

Heat a generous splash of olive oil in a large heavy-based casserole over a medium heat. Season the beef with salt and pepper, then working in batches, add it to the casserole until nicely browned on all sides. Transfer to a plate with a slotted spoon.

Add the rashers and fry for a few minutes, until golden and crisp. Use the slotted spoon again to transfer to the plate with the beef.

Add the onion (and another splash of oil if needed) and cook for 8–10 minutes, until softened. Add the garlic and cinnamon stick and cook for 1 minute more, just until the garlic is fragrant.

Pour in the red wine and increase the heat to high to let it bubble up and deglaze the casserole, stirring up any browned bits. Add 600ml of the stock and bring to a boil, then add the beef and rashers back in, reduce the heat, cover the casserole with a lid and simmer for 2 hours, stirring occasionally. Check on it now and then and top up with more chicken stock if necessary so that the beef always stays submerged.

Add the carrots, cover the casserole again and cook for a further 40 minutes, until the beef is meltingly tender.

Finish with the sliced spring onions, kale and a few cubes of butter. Cook for a few minutes, until the kale has just wilted. Serve with creamy mashed potatoes.

Beef and Guinness pie
with champ and minted greens

Gareth Mullins, The Marker Hotel

In my family, food is a massive part of our lives – we love to spend time cooking and eating together. The table is the heart of our home. It's where we share laughs and conversations and make all our decisions. This pie is perfect to put in the middle of the table to enjoy on a Sunday afternoon or if you are feeding a larger group of family or friends.

Serves 4

2 tbsp olive oil

4 beef cheeks or 1.2kg stewing beef, trimmed and diced (ask your butcher to trim off any sinew and dice the beef cheeks for you)

salt and freshly ground black pepper

100g butter

2 red onions, diced

2 carrots, diced

3 celery sticks, diced

2 garlic cloves, diced

1 tbsp plain flour

1 x 400g tin of chopped tomatoes

100g chestnut mushrooms, sliced

2 bottles of Guinness or stout

2 bay leaves

2 sprigs of fresh thyme, leaves picked

1 sheet of ready-rolled all-butter puff pastry, thawed if frozen

2 egg yolks, beaten

Preheat the oven to 160°C (140°C fan).

Heat the oil in a large heavy-based casserole over a medium-high heat. Season the beef generously with salt and pepper, then working in batches, add it to the casserole to sear on all sides. Be sure to get plenty of colour on the beef, as this will give the filling more flavour. Remove the beef with a slotted spoon and set aside on a plate.

Melt the butter in the same casserole, then add the onions, carrots and celery and sauté for about 10 minutes, until soft. Add the garlic and cook for 1 minute, just until fragrant. Stir in the flour and cook for 1 minute more. Add the beef back in along with the tomatoes, mushrooms, stout, bay leaves and thyme. Bring to a boil, then cover the casserole with a lid and transfer to the preheated oven.

Cook in the oven for 3 hours, until the beef is soft and tender. Spoon everything into a baking dish set on a baking tray (to make it easier to get the pie in and out of the oven) and allow to cool.

Roll out the sheet of puff pastry to fit the top of your dish, then place it on top of the cooled filling.

Increase the oven temperature to 180°C (160°C fan). Brush the top of the pastry with the beaten egg yolks. Transfer the pie to the oven and bake for 30–40 minutes, until the pastry is golden brown and the filling is piping hot.

Meanwhile, to make the champ, boil the potatoes until cooked through, then drain and put back in the pot on the hob for 2 minutes to ensure all the water has evaporated. Mash until smooth. >>

For the champ:

1kg potatoes, peeled

50g butter

1 bunch of spring onions, finely chopped

100ml cream

For the minted greens:

peas, asparagus, kale, broccoli or whatever fresh green vegetables you have

a knob of butter

1 sprig of fresh mint, leaves picked and roughly chopped

Melt the butter in a separate pan over a medium heat. Add the spring onions and sauté for a few minutes, until soft. Add the cream and season with salt and pepper, then fold this through the mashed potatoes.

I like to prep and blanch the greens in plenty of boiling salted water for 3 minutes, then plunge them into lots of iced water to stop the cooking process and ensure they stay green and vibrant. When cooled, strain and set aside.

When you're ready to serve, put the greens back in a pan of boiling water for just 1 minute to heat through, then strain. Toss in the butter and mint and season with salt and pepper.

Serve the beef and Guinness pie straight to the table with bowls of the champ and minted greens on the side for everyone to help themselves.

{tip}

You can make the pie the day before, up to the point where you cool the filling. Cover it with the pastry, brush it with the beaten egg yolks and bake it in the oven on the day.

'I was homeless for many years and getting the **home** from Peter McVerry Trust means a lot. I have my own key and my own personal **space**, which I **love**. I would be lost only for Peter McVerry Trust. I get a lot of **support**, 110% from all the staff.'

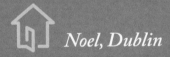 *Noel, Dublin*

Chicken

Chicken, turnip and barley stew

Gaz Smith, Michael's, Big Mike's and Little Mike's

This is my go-to dish when I feel a bit muggy and have had a load of crazy days in a row. I always crave it when I feel a bit tired and 'off' in general. When I eat this stew, I just feel good – it's comfort food in its purest form. More importantly, I also feel great the next day because it's so easy to digest and barley is so soothing. This stew is my little secret weapon. And it's so easy to make too. I chuck everything in the pressure cooker at home and it cooks in no time. If you're going to use a pressure cooker, you can skip the entire method and just chuck in the whole lot, following the instructions on your cooker. By the time I have a shower and get back downstairs in my Nigella-esque silk pyjamas, it's done and ready.

Serves 4

vegetable oil

1.5kg chicken thighs, bone in and skin on

3 small brown onions, diced

3 small carrots, diced

3 celery sticks, diced

3 large Rooster potatoes, peeled and diced

½ small turnip, peeled and diced

3 garlic cloves, finely chopped

salt and freshly ground black pepper

1.5 litres chicken stock

1 large leek, sliced into 2mm-thick rings

150g pearl barley

4–5 sprigs of fresh thyme

a large handful of fresh curly parsley, finely chopped

Place a very large pot over a high heat along with a good glug of oil.

Add your chicken thighs in batches and brown them off, making sure you get a gorgeous brown crust on each piece. As each thigh crisps up, remove it from the pot and rest it on a baking tray. Continue cooking until all your thighs are brown.

To the same pot (which now has lovely crisp chicken bits on its bottom), add your onions, carrots, celery, potatoes, turnip and garlic along with three good pinches of salt. Turn down the heat to medium to sweat off all the veg for 10–15 minutes.

Add your stock and give it all a good stir, then add your browned chicken thighs back to the pot and simmer for 25 minutes.

After 25 minutes, add the leek and barley. Give the whole lot another really good stir and simmer for another 30 minutes, until the leek and barley are cooked. Season to taste with salt and pepper.

Right at the end, add the leaves from the thyme stalks and most of the chopped curly parsley, holding some back for serving.

This is best served warm rather than hot. Leave it for half an hour and all those flavours will just relax into each other. Sprinkle the last bits of chopped parsley on top right before serving. Slurp it down and try to remember that everything will be okay.

Sopas

Richie Castillo, Bahay

I have fond memories of my father making this for my lunch when I was growing up. He would always leave a pot on the stove for everyone to help themselves. This was and still is my go-to comfort dish. Sopas translates to soup and it is essentially the Filipino version of chicken soup.

Serves 4–6

1.2 litres chicken stock

3 chicken breasts

30g butter

1 large onion, finely diced

4 garlic cloves, minced

3 carrots, finely diced

1 celery stick, finely diced

300g macaroni

140g napa cabbage, sliced

100ml milk

100ml cream

1 tsp salt

¼ tsp ground white pepper

Bring the chicken stock to the boil in a large saucepan, then reduce the heat to medium. Add the chicken breasts and simmer for 8–10 minutes, until they are fully cooked through. Remove from the stock and allow to cool a little, then shred with a fork. Make sure to keep the stock.

Melt the butter in a large pot over a medium heat, then throw in your onion and garlic and a pinch of salt. Cook for about 5 minutes, until lightly browned. Throw your carrots and celery into the pot with another small pinch of salt and cook for 2 minutes. Add the reserved chicken stock.

Bring the stock to the boil, then add your macaroni. Check the packet instructions and set a timer for 2 minutes less than the stated cooking time. When the timer goes off, add the shredded chicken along with the cabbage, milk, cream and the seasoning. Continue to boil until the liquid has thickened and the macaroni has fully cooked. Taste and adjust the seasoning, then divide between bowls to serve.

Chicken noodle soup

Kristin Jensen, Nine Bean Rows

Chicken soup is one of those things everyone should know how to make. You shouldn't be able to leave school without knowing how to at least roast a chicken, make chicken soup and cook yourself an omelette. This recipe is for making stock and soup from scratch, but if you've roasted a chicken, make stock with the carcass to extract every last bit of value and goodness from it. The stock will keep in the freezer for three months, ready for those times when a bowl of homemade chicken noodle soup and a hug is the only thing that will do.

Serves 4

For the stock:

1 large whole chicken

1 onion, unpeeled and quartered through the root end

3 carrots, scrubbed well, unpeeled and cut in half

3 celery stalks, cut in half (leaves included)

1 head of garlic, cut in half around its middle to expose all the cloves

10 black peppercorns

2 bay leaves

1 bunch of fresh parsley, stalks only

1 tbsp salt

To make the stock, put the chicken in a large stockpot, one big enough to hold it and all the vegetables plus plenty of water. Add all the remaining stock ingredients, then pour over enough cold water to cover the chicken. Cover the pot and bring to a boil, then reduce it to a steady simmer and let it bubble away, covered, for 90 minutes to ensure the chicken gets fully cooked.

Partially uncover the pot and continue to let it simmer for a further 30–60 minutes to let the stock reduce a bit and get a more concentrated flavour. Don't let the stock boil for more than 3 hours max, though, or the texture of the chicken will get too soft.

Carefully remove the chicken from the pot onto a plate and allow it to cool. Strain the stock through a sieve into a large bowl, pressing on the vegetables with the back of a spoon to get as much liquid as possible out of them, then discard them. If you're making the stock ahead of time, cover the bowl with cling film and put it in the fridge overnight to allow the fat to congeal on the top, then skim it off.

Once the chicken is cool enough to handle, discard the skin and bones and any other unsavoury bits, then dice or shred the chicken. You'll only need half of it for the soup, so save the rest for adding to pasta, stir-fries, salads, lentils, risotto, chicken salad sandwiches – you get the idea. >>

For the soup:

1–2 tbsp olive oil

1 onion, finely chopped

3 carrots, peeled and finely diced

2 celery stalks, finely diced

salt and freshly ground black pepper

2–3 garlic cloves, finely chopped

1.5 litres of your homemade chicken stock

200g macaroni

a handful of fresh parsley, chopped

To serve:

crusty bread

To make the soup, heat the olive oil in a large pot over a medium-low heat. Add the onion, carrots and celery along with a good pinch of salt (to keep the onion from browning) and some pepper. Cover the pot with a lid and sweat the veg for 10–15 minutes, stirring occasionally, until they have softened but not coloured. Add the garlic and cook for 1 minute more, just until fragrant.

Add a few handfuls of the cooked shredded chicken and 1.5 litres of the stock and bring to a boil, then reduce to a lively simmer and add the pasta. A lot of chicken noodle soup recipes call for wide pasta noodles, but I like to use macaroni because it's easier to scoop up with a spoon. If you're not feeling the best to begin with, you want the act of eating your soup to be as undemanding as possible. Cook for 10–15 minutes, until the pasta is cooked through. Add the parsley at the last minute.

Ladle the soup into bowls. Pass around plenty of crusty bread to mop up every last drop of the nourishing stock. Serve steaming hot and feel better soon.

{*tip*}

If you're very organised, prep the vegetables for the soup before you make the stock so that you can add the carrot peelings, celery leaves and onion and garlic skins to the stock pot.

You can freeze any leftover chicken stock for up to three months.

'My **home** was always my source of energy and calmness. It was like my **shelter**, where I could always escape from a busy life and get some **rest**. I moved to the capital of Ukraine five years ago, but I always found time to go home to my hometown, Kryvyi Rih, where my mom and our dogs, cats and chickens were waiting for me. Being at home felt like returning to my childhood, where I always felt **safe** and **protected**. But when the war started, we lost our safe place.'

Daria, Ukraine
Daria fled the war in Ukraine in 2022. She first come in contact with Peter McVerry Trust through International Protection Accommodation Services (IPAS). Since then she has moved into pledged accommodation with her mother in Dublin and now works in the Peter McVerry Trust Pledge team, helping others to find a home.

Coronation chicken flatbreads

Graham Herterich, The Bakery

To me, home is a feeling – feelings from my childhood of comfort, safety and togetherness that as an adult I have been able to find in more places than just the traditional home. I can get that feeling of comfort sitting in a café having a coffee with my sister or I can get that feeling of safety knowing that my friends or family are at the other end of the phone if I need them. The feeling of togetherness comes from sharing a table and food with family, be it my biological family or my logical family (the people who I have chosen to be part of my life).

Serves 4

For the flatbreads:

350g self-raising flour, plus extra for dusting

350g Greek yogurt

4 spring onions, finely chopped

salt and freshly ground black pepper

For the coronation chicken:

8 chicken thighs, trimmed of skin and fat

1 tbsp sunflower oil

1 tbsp curry powder

For the sauce:

1 tbsp sunflower oil

1 small onion, thinly sliced

2 tsp curry powder

50g dried apricots, thinly sliced

2 tbsp mayonnaise

2 tbsp Greek yogurt

1 tbsp mango chutney

For the salad:

a few handfuls of mixed leaves

20 cherry tomatoes, cut into quarters

8 fresh apricots, cut into wedges

To make the flatbreads, put the flour, yogurt, spring onions and a pinch of salt and pepper in a large bowl and mix together with a spoon to form a dough. Dust a clean work surface with a little flour, then tip the dough out onto the counter and knead for a minute or so to bring it all together. Put the dough in a flour-dusted bowl, cover with a clean tea towel and leave to rest for 30 minutes at room temperature.

Divide the dough in half, then divide each half into four equal-sized pieces to make eight flatbreads. Roll each piece into a 12cm round.

Put a frying pan over a high heat without any oil. Once it's hot, cook each round for 1–2 minutes on each side, until puffed up and colouring nicely. Wrap the flatbreads in a clean tea towel to keep warm.

Preheat the oven to 220°C (200°C fan). Line a baking tray with non-stick baking paper.

Rub the chicken with the oil, curry powder and some salt and pepper. Arrange on the lined tray and cook in the preheated oven for 20 minutes. Allow to cool, then shred the chicken.

To make the sauce, heat the oil in a saucepan over a medium heat. Add the onion and fry for a few minutes, until golden, then add the curry powder and cook gently for 1 minute. Remove the pan from the heat and allow to cool before stirring in the rest of the sauce ingredients.

To assemble, spread the coronation sauce over the flatbreads. Top each one with mixed leaves, quartered cherry tomatoes and fresh apricots, then put some shredded chicken on top of the salad. Serve any extra sauce on the side. Alternatively, this works equally well served in large bowls and platters where everyone can help themselves.

Cantonese lemon chicken

Kwanghi Chan, Bites by Kwanghi

I left Hong Kong when I was eight years old, so home has always been Buncrana in Donegal. It's where I helped my grandmother to cook family dinners, making dumplings, soups and Chinese stews, surrounded by the smells of home cooking. Even now, whenever I walk into a restaurant that is serving the same dishes that my grandmother used to cook, it brings me right back. This Cantonese lemon chicken is one of the first dishes I learned to make working in my uncle's Chinese restaurant. Today, I love cooking it for my children.

Serves 2

2 tbsp light soy sauce

1 tbsp Shaoxing wine
(Chinese cooking wine)

1 egg white

330g chicken fillets , cut into strips
3mm thick

200g potato starch

vegetable oil, for deep-frying

For the sauce:

200ml chicken stock

4 tbsp honey

1½ tbsp light soy sauce

2 tsp potato starch

2 lemons – zest of 1, juice of 2

1 tbsp vegetable oil

1 garlic clove, crushed

1 tsp finely grated fresh ginger

To serve:

boiled jasmine rice

toasted sesame seeds

1–2 spring onions, thinly sliced

Put the soy sauce, cooking wine and egg white in a large bowl and whisk together to break up the egg white. Add the chicken fillets, tossing to coat, then set aside to marinate for 20 minutes.

Put the 200g potato starch in a large tray or bowl. Take the chicken pieces out of the marinade, shaking off any excess. Dredge the chicken in the potato starch, pressing to form a craggy coating on each piece.

Heat the oil in a deep-fryer to 170°C. Alternatively, fill a wok or saucepan about one-third full of vegetable oil and heat over a high heat. If you don't have a thermometer to test the temperature of the oil, you can tell it's hot enough for frying when a wooden chopstick dipped into the oil forms small bubbles.

Shake off any excess potato starch from the chicken pieces. Working in batches if necessary so that you don't overcrowd your deep-fryer or wok, fry the chicken pieces for about 3 minutes, until golden and cooked through. Drain on kitchen paper or in a sieve set over a bowl.

To make the sauce, mix together the chicken stock, honey, soy sauce and potato starch in a jug. In a separate bowl, mix together the lemon zest and juice. Set both aside.

Heat the tablespoon of oil in a clean wok or saucepan over a medium-high heat. Add the garlic and ginger and cook for about 10 seconds, just until fragrant. Add the chicken stock mixture and cook for 2–3 minutes, until the sauce starts to thicken, then add the lemon zest and juice. Cook for another 30 seconds, until the sauce has thickened a little more. If it's still a bit runny, add another teaspoon of potato starch. Add the fried chicken pieces and toss until evenly coated in the sauce.

Serve the chicken on a bed of jasmine rice and garnish with toasted sesame seeds and spring onions.

Roman chicken and chips
with rosemary and thyme

Darina Allen, Ballymaloe Cookery School

My family and friends love me to cook this dish for them, a whole roasting tray of crispy chicken and potatoes, perfumed with rosemary and thyme leaves. My lips are smacking just thinking about it.

Serves 8–10

2kg organic, free-range chicken thighs, drumsticks and wings

flaky sea salt and freshly ground black pepper

2–3 tbsp fresh thyme leaves

1–2 tbsp chopped fresh rosemary

1.1kg (about 10 large) potatoes

extra virgin olive oil, to drizzle

250g onions, sliced

Preheat the oven to 230°C (210°C fan).

Season the chicken heavily with salt and pepper. Put into a large bowl and scatter with most of the thyme leaves and chopped rosemary, reserving some for the potatoes. Toss well.

Peel the potatoes and cut into 1cm-thick chips. Dry and season well with salt, pepper and the reserved thyme and chopped rosemary. Add to the bowl with the chicken, drizzle with extra virgin olive oil and toss once again.

Scatter the sliced onions over the base of one large roasting tin (approx. 37cm x 31cm x 2cm) or two smaller tins (approx. 30cm x 20cm x 2.5cm). Arrange the chicken and potatoes haphazardly on top, making sure that the potatoes are popping up. Drizzle with a little more olive oil.

Roast in the preheated oven for 45 minutes to 1 hour, until the chicken is cooked through and the chips are crispy at the edges. (Organic chicken pieces are larger, so the cooking time can be up to 1¼ hours.)

Serve from the tin, family style, with a good green salad and several vegetables of your choice if you wish.

{tip}

You can add a little hot homemade chicken stock at the end if the dish needs a little more juice.

Roast chicken thighs and potatoes
with tomatoes, olives and feta

Anthony O'Toole, food and travel advisor

One-pan dinners are a go-to in my household. They are quick to prepare, create very little washing up and are a crowd-pleaser for when I'm entertaining colleagues, family and friends. They are versatile as you can change the ingredients with the seasons or depending on what you have to hand. Instead of tomatoes and olives, you could add half a bag of frozen peas at the end – peas, thyme, oregano and feta go so well together. If you don't like feta, you can leave it out or try some full-fat ricotta. This dish can also be made with firm white fish like halibut, haddock or cod. Just add the fish after cooking the potatoes for 40 minutes so that you roast the fish for only 10 minutes at the end. There are always chicken thighs in my freezer as one of Ireland's best chicken farmers, Regan Organic Farm, is just a short drive away from where I live.

Serves 4–6

800g small baby salad potatoes (I recommend the Charlotte variety), halved lengthways

8 chicken thighs or legs, bone in and skin on

2 red onions, peeled and each cut into 6 wedges

1 head of garlic, cloves separated, peeled and kept whole

a handful of fresh thyme leaves, roughly chopped

a handful of fresh oregano leaves or rosemary, chopped, plus extra to garnish

3 tbsp olive oil

flaky sea salt and freshly ground black pepper

1 unwaxed lemon, cut into 6 wedges

100ml white vermouth or white wine

25 cherry tomatoes

20 fat green Greek or Spanish olives, stoned

100g feta cheese, roughly crumbled

1 tbsp extra virgin olive oil

Preheat the oven to 200°C (180°C fan).

Put the potatoes, chicken, red onions and garlic cloves in a large roasting tray (the biggest tray you have). Add the thyme, oregano or rosemary, olive oil and a good pinch of flaky sea salt and freshly ground black pepper. Toss together to ensure everything is evenly coated with the seasoned, herby olive oil. Spread out in an even layer, making sure the chicken skin is facing up. Some chicken can sit on top of the potatoes and onions. Add the lemon wedges around the chicken.

Roast in the preheated oven for 35 minutes, then remove the tin from the oven and increase the temperature to 220°C (200°C fan). Add the vermouth or white wine, cherry tomatoes and olives. Place back in the oven and cook for 15 minutes more, until the chicken skin is golden and crisp.

Remove from the oven and sprinkle over the feta and some fresh oregano. Drizzle with the tablespoon of extra virgin olive oil and season with a pinch of flaky sea salt.

Serve in the middle of the table. Depending on the occasion or time of year, you can serve this with a tomato salad on the side, some mixed lettuce leaves or both.

Creamy chicken korma

Neven Maguire, MacNean House and Restaurant

Home has always being a huge part of my life, from growing up in a family of nine to my home now with my wife, Amelda and my twins, Connor and Lucia. Sitting down to chat and enjoy a delicious home-cooked meal together at our kitchen table is the most important part of my day.

This korma is a real favourite in our house and I make it all the time for the twins. It can be made ahead of time and keeps well in the fridge. It's also a really versatile recipe – sometimes I add diced monkfish and prawns instead of the chicken and pack it with vegetables like cauliflower, butternut squash and peppers.

Serves 4

2 tbsp rapeseed oil

2 onions, finely chopped

2 garlic cloves, crushed

1 green chilli, deseeded and finely chopped (optional)

2 tsp finely grated fresh ginger

1 tsp garam masala

1 tsp ground turmeric

¼ tsp chilli powder (optional)

salt and freshly ground black pepper

1 x 400g tin of chopped tomatoes

2 tbsp mango chutney, plus extra to serve

1 tsp tomato purée

4 tbsp water

1 x 400ml tin of coconut milk

4 x 175g boneless, skinless chicken breasts, cut into 2.5cm cubes

To serve:

steamed basmati rice

a handful of fresh coriander leaves

warm naan

Heat the oil in a large pan over a medium-heat heat and fry the onions and garlic for 6–8 minutes, until golden brown. Stir in the green chilli (if using) and ginger and cook for 1 minute, stirring.

Add the garam masala, turmeric, chilli powder (if using) and a pinch of salt and cook for another minute, stirring. Add the tinned tomatoes, chutney, tomato purée and water. Stir well to combine, then bring to a fast simmer for 5 minutes, stirring occasionally, until the sauce is so well reduced that it's almost sticking to the bottom of the pan.

Stir in the coconut milk, then the chicken. Slowly bring to the boil, then reduce the heat and simmer gently for 10–15 minutes, until the chicken is cooked through and completely tender. Season to taste.

To serve, arrange the basmati rice and chicken korma on warmed plates and scatter over the coriander leaves. Place the naan in a separate dish to hand around at the table along with the mango chutney.

Easy chicken curry

Santosh Thomas, 3 Leaves

The curry leaves and coconut milk in this dish remind me of home. For a busy household like ours, this recipe is a regular in our meal prep rotation. I make the recipe up to the step before adding the coconut milk, then I put it in the freezer until I need it. Defrost it and complete the last step for a quick and easy chicken curry for a busy weekday dinner.

Serves 2–3

3 tbsp sunflower oil

¼ tsp mustard seeds

3 spring onions, chopped

1 medium tomato, chopped

4–5 curry leaves

500g skinless, boneless chicken thighs, cut into bite-sized pieces

2 tbsp ground coriander

½ tsp Kashmiri chilli powder

½ tsp salt

¼ tsp ground turmeric

¼ tsp fried garlic

280ml water

1 x 400ml tin of coconut milk

¼ tsp caster sugar

¼ tsp lemon juice

To serve:

steamed basmati rice

warm naan

Heat the sunflower oil in a deep saucepan over a low heat. Add the mustard seeds and let them crackle, then add the spring onions and cook for 3–4 minutes, until they are translucent.

Add the chopped tomato and the curry leaves. Increase the heat to medium and cook for a few minutes. As soon as the tomato turns soft, add the chicken, coriander, chilli powder, salt, turmeric and fried garlic. Mix together until the chicken thighs are well coated with the sauce.

Add the water and cover the pan with a lid. Let this cook on a medium-low heat for 25–30 minutes, stirring occasionally, until the water has evaporated to produce a dry, thick sauce.

Stir in the coconut milk and simmer for 2 minutes to heat through. Finish the curry with the sugar and lemon juice. Taste and adjust the salt as required.

Serve with steamed basmati rice and warm naan.

{tip}

You can adjust the consistency of the curry by adding hot water as required.

Soy lemon chicken

Eva Pau, Asia Market

This recipe for soy lemon chicken isn't what you would normally find in a typical Chinese restaurant – rather, it was inspired by the way my grandmother Nancy made it. It uses whole chicken thighs and lots of sliced lemon and has a beautiful sticky sauce. This dish is a firm favourite with my family at home.

Serves 4

800g chicken thighs, bone in
and skin on

5 tbsp water

5 tbsp light soy sauce

3 tbsp dark soy sauce

1 tbsp Shaoxing wine
(Chinese cooking wine)

1 tsp sesame oil

1 large lemon, sliced

2 medium-sized pieces of Chinese
brown sugar, broken into pieces,
or 3 tbsp brown sugar

vegetable or sunflower oil, for cooking

To serve:

boiled jasmine rice

fresh coriander leaves

1 fresh green chilli, deseeded and
thinly sliced

2–3 spring onions, thinly sliced
at an angle (optional)

toasted sesame seeds (optional)

Put the chicken in a large sealable container. Pour in the water, light and dark soy sauce, cooking wine and sesame oil, then put the lemon slices and sugar on top. Put the lid on and shake it a few times to coat the chicken. Marinate in the fridge for at least 2 hours or overnight is best.

Heat a little oil in a large non-stick frying pan over a medium heat. While that's heating up, use a small sharp knife to pierce the chicken thighs so that the sauce will infuse the meat. Add the chicken to the pan skin side down so that it gets brown and crisp. Cook for 5 minutes, then turn over and cook for 5 minutes more.

Add the lemon slices and sugar on top of the chicken, then pour in the marinade. Cover the pan with a lid, reduce the heat to low and cook for 20 minutes, until the chicken is completely cooked through. Remove the lid and allow the sauce to reduce until it's nice and sticky.

Serve the chicken on a bed of boiled jasmine rice and scatter over some fresh coriander leaves, green chilli, sliced spring onions and toasted sesame seeds (if using).

{*tip*}

You can watch a video of Eva making this dish on YouTube.
Search for 'Cooking demo – lemon soy chicken with Eva Pau'.

Barbecued chicken
with beer butter, grilled corn and potato flatbreads

Paula McIntyre, chef, food writer and broadcaster

I live in a small bungalow on the north coast and have a cabin in the garden with all my cooking gadgets, a cooking island and a fridge full of local beers, wine and many preserves and ferments. I love being in there with nothing else to do but pour a glass of wine, roll up some pasta, make some tortellinis filled with whatever is in season and play some tunes. One of my favourite things to eat is a good roast chicken, anointed with butter to crisp perfection. Ideally I'd rip it up and use good bread to mop up all the juices. This recipe is a souped-up riff on that. The chicken is rubbed with spices, basted with a beer butter and served with potato flatbreads to soak up the juices, with some corn on the cob treated the same way as the chicken. It's a tactile dish, perfect for serving to friends who don't mind getting down and dirty with their food. It would be rude not to have some local brews to wash it all down.

Serves 4–6

1 x 1.2kg chicken, spatchcocked (ask your butcher to do this for you)

1 tbsp Dijon mustard

For the beer butter:

1 tbsp oil

1 small onion, finely chopped

2 garlic cloves, finely chopped

200ml Irish pale ale

1 tbsp honey

1 tbsp tomato purée

150g butter, softened

For the spice rub:

1 tbsp soft brown sugar

2 tsp onion powder

1 tsp ground cumin

1 tsp smoked paprika

1 tsp English mustard powder

1 tsp salt

First make the beer butter. Heat the oil in a small saucepan over a medium heat. Add the onion and garlic and cook for 5–8 minutes, until golden. Add the ale, honey and tomato purée and bring to a boil to reduce to a thick consistency. Remove the pan from the heat and allow to cool, then blend with the butter. You'll have more than you need but it will keep in the fridge for a week or you can freeze it.

Heat up your barbecue.

Mix together all the spice rub ingredients. Brush the chicken all over with the Dijon mustard, then sprinkle three-quarters of the spice rub over the top (keep the rest for the corn).

Put the chicken on the grill, breast side down. Sear until golden brown, then turn it over and put a lid on the barbecue. If it's a gas barbecue, lower the heat; if it's coals, close the vents to lower the temperature. After 30 minutes, start brushing the chicken with the butter and turn it a couple times. It should take about 1 hour for the chicken to cook through. If you have a temperature probe, the legs should read at least 75°C when it's inserted. Remove the chicken from the barbecue and allow to rest, then slice the chicken breast and remove the legs to serve whole. >>

Potato flatbreads:

100g cold mashed potato

250g self-raising flour

1 tsp salt

4 tbsp natural yogurt

2 tbsp oil

100ml warm water

For the grilled corn:

4 corn on the cob

1 tbsp oil

While the chicken is cooking, make the flatbreads. Rub the mash into the flour. Add the salt, then mix in the yogurt, oil and just enough of the water to make a soft dough. Divide into six even portions and roll each one out as thinly as possible. Cook on a hot pan (or the barbecue after the chicken is done) for about 1 minute on each side. Wrap up in a clean tea towel to keep warm.

While the chicken is resting, cook the corn in boiling salted water for 2 minutes. Drain and brush with the oil and the reserved spice rub. Cook on the grill until scorched slightly – keep moving it around the grill. Brush with a little butter before serving.

To serve, brush the carved barbecued chicken with more beer butter. Serve with the grilled corn on the side and the flatbreads to mop up all the juices from the chicken.

'A **home** is where we make our memories with the people we care about. We are so **grateful** and **proud** of our home. It's a place for our **love**, **hopes** and **dreams**. To us, **family** is everything – loving unconditionally and being there for each other no matter what challenges we face.

Respect, **encouragement**, **care** and **pride** are all words I'd use to describe our family and I can only hope my children grow up knowing the importance of it.'

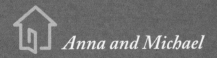

Anna and Michael

Batata sofrito

Dvir Nusery, Mezze

This simple, comforting dish often appears at our family dinners for Shabbat on Friday night, which is when my family in Israel gathers to eat together. When I cook it, I am reminded of home. It's one of those recipes that has been passed down from generation to generation. Its origins most likely come from Spain with the word *sofrito*, which means 'to fry lightly', mixed with the Arabic word *batata*, which means 'potato'. The name of the dish tells of the journey my family made to share a meal together.

My mother makes this dish, having learned it from her mother-in-law. My mother's mother died when she was young and she was fostered by another family. Life was tough and food was scarce. When my mother married, her mother-in-law took her under her wing and taught her the family recipes and everything she knew about cooking. For my mother, cooking is not something she enjoys but she does it out of love to gather her family together for a shared meal.

Serves 4–6

oil, for frying

600g potatoes (I prefer Maris Piper), cut into halves or quarters, but ideally batons or chips

4 free-range chicken legs, separated into drumsticks and thighs

1 tsp ground turmeric

1 tsp salt

¼ tsp ground black pepper

To serve:

salad

boiled rice

Heat a little oil in a wide saucepan on a medium heat. Add the potatoes and lightly fry until just golden – you don't need to cook them through fully at this stage. Drain on kitchen paper and set aside.

Add the chicken pieces to the pan and brown them on all sides. Add the turmeric, salt and pepper and fry for a further 1–2 minutes. Add enough water to cover the chicken, then cover the pan and bring to the boil. Reduce the heat to low and cook for 45 minutes, until the chicken is tender. Add the potatoes back to the pan and cook for a further 15 minutes, until soft.

Spoon onto a large serving platter or into a large wide bowl to share with your family or guests. We usually have this dish with salad and rice.

Chicken, mushroom and leek pie

Danni Barry, Ballynahinch Castle

Home cooking makes me think of generous portions and steaming bowls of hearty soups or stews. Food that warms you up from the inside out, cooked by someone who wants to look after you rather than impress you. Food to set you up for the day.

Growing up on a farm, there were always plenty of people to feed at our table and even the humblest offerings were always appreciated. This recipe is just that, using leftover chicken from a Sunday roast and making what is essentially a stew. The addition of double cream and buttery pastry elevates it to a dinner table centrepiece. Also, I just love a pie. For me, it is the ultimate comfort food.

Serves 4

2 x 350g sheets of ready-rolled all-butter puff pastry

1 tbsp olive oil

1 small onion, diced

1 large leek, washed, trimmed and sliced

130g brown mushrooms

400ml chicken stock

200ml double cream

400g leftover cooked chicken (or 2 cooked breasts), chopped

1 tbsp chopped fresh tarragon

1 tbsp chopped fresh flat-leaf parsley

salt and freshly ground black pepper

1 egg, beaten

Preheat the oven to 200°C (180°C fan). Line a pie plate with one sheet of the puff pastry, then place the pie plate on a baking tray to make it easier to get the pie in and out of the oven.

Heat the olive oil in a large saucepan over a medium heat. Add the onion and leek and cook for 1 minute. Add the mushrooms and cook for another minute, then add the chicken stock and double cream. Bring to a boil, then lower the heat a bit and reduce the liquid until it starts to thicken slightly.

Add the cooked chicken, tarragon and parsley. Season with salt and pepper and stir thoroughly. Once the chicken has heated through, remove the pan from the heat. Spoon the pie mixture into the lined pie plate, filling it right up.

Cut the remaining sheet of puff pastry down to size so that it covers your pie plate, then place it on top. Cut around the side of the plate to remove the excess, then crimp the pastry at the edges to seal. Brush the beaten egg all over the pastry to glaze.

Place the dish in the preheated oven and bake for 30 minutes, until the pastry is golden brown and cooked.

Remove from the oven and serve immediately.

Pork

Bacon and cabbage

Wade Murphy, 1826 Adare

Bacon and cabbage is my favourite home-cooked meal. We cook it at home on our days off at least once a fortnight. No matter where I was living or working in the world, whenever I came home to Gorey this was the first thing my mam would cook for me. Now the big argument is parsley sauce or no parsley sauce.

Serves 4–6

1kg collar of bacon

12 floury potatoes, such as Kerr's Pink

2 heads of sweetheart or Hispi cabbage

1 turnip, peeled and cut into large wedges

50g butter, plus extra for the cabbage and potatoes

salt and freshly ground black pepper

For the parsley sauce:

25g butter

25g plain flour

300ml full-fat milk

salt and ground white pepper

4 tbsp chopped fresh curly parsley

½ tsp Dijon mustard

First soak the bacon in cold water for at least 1 hour, but ideally overnight. Drain and rinse.

Put the rinsed bacon in a large pot, cover in cold water and bring slowly to a boil. Once it comes to the boil, drain all the water, cover again with cold water and bring to a boil again. Once it's boiling, turn the heat down to a nice rolling boil and cook for 1 hour 15 minutes. The recommended cooking time for bacon is 45 minutes per kg plus 20 minutes extra at the end, so a 1kg collar of bacon will definitely be cooked right through in the amount of time given here.

Towards the end of the cooking time for the bacon, cook the whole, unpeeled potatoes in a separate pot of boiling salted water until tender and their skins burst. Drain and return the potatoes to the pot to dry out and keep warm.

Trim the outer leaves from the cabbage and cut it into quarters. Discard the outer leaves. About 30 minutes before the bacon is cooked, add the turnip wedges to the pot with the bacon, then 10 minutes after that, add the cabbage quarters. Stir, cover and continue to cook gently until the turnip, cabbage and bacon are all cooked.

Take the bacon out of the pot and allow to rest in a warm place.

Strain the cabbage and transfer it to a platter. Keep 300ml of the cooking water for the parsley sauce. It should not be salty, as you rinsed the bacon before cooking. Add a knob of butter to the cabbage and season with salt and pepper. Set aside to keep warm. >>

Remove the turnip from the cooking water and pat it dry. Melt the butter in a frying pan over a medium-high heat, then add the turnip wedges. Cook until they are nicely caramelised, then season with salt and pepper.

Meanwhile, to make the parsley sauce, melt the butter in a saucepan over a medium-high heat. Stir in the flour and cook for 1–2 minutes. Take the pan off the heat and gradually stir in the milk and the reserved 300ml of the bacon cooking liquid to get a smooth sauce. Return the pan to the heat and bring to a boil, stirring all the time. Reduce the heat and simmer gently for 8–9 minutes, then season with salt and white pepper. Stir in the parsley and Dijon mustard.

Carve the bacon and serve with the cabbage, turnip, floury potatoes and parsley sauce. I love to melt cold butter on top of the floury potatoes too.

'In a **community** that loves one another, there should be no one poor (unless all are poor), there should be no one homeless, no one lonely, no one sick or alone without visitors, no one in prison who has been abandoned and written off, no one rejected or marginalised.'

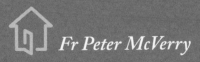

Fr Peter McVerry

Barbecued pork chops
with mustard mash

Rick Higgins, Higgins Family Butcher

My mam and dad both worked full time in our butcher shop so time was always precious, but they made a big deal of family mealtimes. I've carried on this tradition with my own children, with mealtimes being the centre of our home – a chance to catch up, chat and maybe argue just a little from time to time.

Serves 4

4 x 300g bone-in pork chops

Hardcore Carnivore Red Dry Rub Seasoning (or your favourite dry rub)

For the mustard mash:

700g Ballymakenny Mayan Gold potatoes (or your favourite potatoes)

50g butter

50ml double cream

2 tbsp wholegrain mustard

For the cognac cream sauce:

20g butter

1 medium onion, finely chopped

1 garlic clove, finely chopped

100ml cognac

300ml double cream

2 tsp wholegrain mustard

salt and ground white pepper

Coat the pork chops in the dry rub seasoning. This can be done up to 1 hour in advance.

Preheat your charcoal barbecue.

Cook the pork chops over a direct heat (ideally around 250°C) until the internal temperature is at least 75°C. Set aside to rest.

Meanwhile, to make the mustard mash, peel the potatoes and cut them into chunks, making sure they are a similar size to avoid uneven cooking. Put in a medium-sized pot, cover with cold water and add a pinch of salt. Bring to a boil, then reduce the heat to a simmer for 15–20 minutes, until the potatoes are cooked through. Drain and return to the dry pot.

Heat the butter and cream in a separate saucepan until the butter has melted. Mash the potatoes with the wholegrain mustard, then gradually stir in the melted butter and cream until the mash is the consistency you like.

Finally, to make the sauce, melt the butter in a saucepan over a medium heat. Add the onion and garlic and cook for 5 minutes, until the onion has softened. Add the cognac to the pan and allow it to flambé (catch fire). When the flame has disappeared, stir in the cream and mustard. Simmer until the sauce coats the back of a spoon, then season with salt and white pepper.

To serve, put a bed of mash on each plate. Put a pork chop on top of the mash, then spoon over the sauce.

Baked sausage meatballs
in tomato sauce

Peter Hannan, Hannan Meats

People, comfort, laughter and food are all important factors in maintaining a happy home. Everybody loves meatballs and they are simplicity itself. Served with a salad, pasta or just a good loaf of bread, they're a winner.

Serves 4

25g butter

½ medium onion, diced

1 fresh chilli, deseeded and finely diced (optional)

2 tbsp chopped fresh flat-leaf parsley

500g sausage meat (Italian sausage if possible)

40g dried breadcrumbs (preferably panko)

1–2 handfuls of grated mozzarella cheese

For the tomato sauce:

2 tbsp olive oil

3 garlic cloves, finely chopped

2 tsp dried oregano

a pinch of dried chilli flakes (optional)

2 x 400g tins of chopped tomatoes

1 bunch of fresh basil, roughly chopped – reserve a few leaves for garnish

To serve:

tomato and onion salad

crusty bread

Start by making the tomato sauce. Heat the oil in a saucepan over a medium heat. Add the garlic, oregano and chilli flakes (if using) and cook for 2 minutes, then add the tomatoes. Bring to a boil, then reduce the heat and simmer for 20 minutes. Allow to cool, then stir in the basil and set aside.

Preheat the oven to 200°C (180°C fan).

To make the meatballs, melt the butter in a small frying pan over a medium heat. Add the onion and cook for 5 minutes, until soft and translucent. Add the chilli (if using) and cook for 2 minutes more, then stir in the parsley. Remove the pan from the heat and allow to cool.

Put the sausage meat in a large bowl with the breadcrumbs and the cooled onion mixture and stir together thoroughly. Divide into 12 x 50g meatballs (about the size of a golf ball).

Spread half of the cooled tomato sauce in the bottom of a baking dish. Add the meatballs in a single layer, then cover with the remaining sauce.

Cook in the preheated oven for 15 minutes. Remove the dish from the oven and cover with grated mozzarella, then return to the oven to cook for another 15 minutes, until the cheese is browned and bubbling.

Allow to stand for 5 minutes, then serve the dish straight to the table with a tomato and onion salad on the side and plenty of crusty bread to mop up all the sauce.

Sausage meatloaf

Suzanne Campbell, writer and broadcaster

Home to me means family sitting around a table sharing food. My mother and grandmothers were all great cooks. They were from farming families, so the quality of food was of huge importance: fresh eggs, home-grown tomatoes, good ham and great baking. Growing up, I came in from school every day to the smell of freshly baked brown bread. It's something I regrettably don't do, but I cook everything from scratch and make sure we have a family meal together every evening. This is where we share our funny stories or frustrations from the day and our plans (and most importantly, make fun of each other).

I first made this recipe as a teenager when I took over making the Christmas stuffing. I started putting in bay leaves and thyme from the garden in our old house and plenty of onion and garlic, then adapted it over the years. Now it's a dish I make throughout the year, mostly in winter, and my children absolutely love it. It's like a huge posh sausage, basically, with a rich, herby smell and texture. It makes a wonderful weekday supper. I serve it with salads, flatbreads or pitta, mashed potatoes and peas, or cold in sandwiches, which is a big lunchtime hit.

Serves 4

a good splash of olive oil

1 medium onion, diced

3 garlic cloves, finely chopped

2 tbsp mixed dried herbs

1 tbsp ground cumin

1 tbsp fresh thyme leaves

1 tbsp fennel seeds

500g good-quality Irish sausage meat

300g breadcrumbs (brown bread is ideal, but white is good too)

½ tsp salt

freshly ground black pepper

Preheat the oven to 200°C (180°C fan). Tear off a large sheet of foil, enough to line your baking tray and also bring it up around the meatloaf to enclose it.

Heat the olive oil in a frying pan over a medium heat. Add the onion and cook for about 10 minutes, until softened and translucent. Add the garlic, mixed dried herbs, cumin, thyme and fennel seeds and cook for 3 minutes more, until softened. Remove the pan from the heat and allow to cool.

Put the sausage meat and the cooled onion mixture in a large bowl along with the breadcrumbs, salt and two good twists of the pepper mill. Using clean hands, mix all the ingredients together, kneading and squeezing the mixture until you have an even consistency of breadcrumbs and sausage meat.

Transfer to the lined baking sheet and form the meatloaf into a roughly rectangular shape, then loosely cover with the overhanging foil to form a tent, crimping the edges tightly to seal. Transfer to the middle or top shelf of the preheated oven and cook for 35 minutes, then unfold the foil and cook for 10–15 minutes more so that the top can brown and the meatloaf is completely cooked through.

Remove from the oven leave to cool a little before cutting into slices to serve.

Smoked ham and leek pie

Olivia Duff, Maperath Farm

This recipe has provided comfort at our table not just on cold, wet days, but also to those who have shared our table who required comfort, like our visiting Ukrainian family. I also take comfort in knowing that we have reared and produced the ham ourselves. We are blessed to have a wonderful butcher in Hugh Maguire (aka 'The Smokin' Butcher') who naturally smokes our rare-breed hams for us at home at Maperath Farm. This pie is the perfect way to use up a baked ham or Christmas ham and we all agree that it's even better the next day.

Serves 6

85g butter

1 tsp rapeseed oil

1 large onion, finely chopped

3 medium-sized leeks, thinly sliced

1 heaped tsp English or French mustard (Graham's Mustard is wonderful)

85g plain flour, plus extra for dusting

300ml chicken stock

50ml double cream

300g cooked smoked ham hock or leg or cooked baked ham, flaked apart

salt and freshly ground black pepper

1 sheet of ready-rolled puff pastry, thawed if frozen

1 egg, beaten

To serve:

green salad

Preheat the oven to 180°C (160°C fan).

Heat the butter and oil in a large frying pan over a medium heat. When the butter has melted, add the onion and cook gently, covered with a lid, for about 10 minutes, until softened and translucent. Add the leeks and cook for a few minutes more, covered, until softened but not coloured.

Add the mustard and then the flour and cook for 1–2 minutes to cook off the raw taste of the flour, then pour in the stock and cream. Add the ham and mix well to combine, then season to taste. Cook for just a couple minutes to marry the flavours together, then take the pan off the heat.

Transfer to a 25cm pie dish and allow to cool before putting on the pastry. (The pie can be prepped in advance and left overnight at this stage to cook the next day.)

Roll out the pastry on a lightly floured surface until it will cover your pie dish. Carefully drape the pastry over the top, pressing to seal the edges, then trim off any excess pastry.

Brush the top of the pie with the beaten egg, then prick with a fork to allow steam to escape. Put the dish on a baking tray to make it easier to get the pie in and out of the oven. Bake in the preheated oven for 45 minutes, until the pastry is golden brown and the filling is bubbling.

Bring the pie to the table to let everyone help themselves. Serve with a simple green salad on the side.

Risotto alla Monzese

Manuela Spinelli, Euro-Toques

I grew up in the province of Monza and Brianza, in the countryside just outside Milan. My grandfather kept rabbits, chickens and pigeons and he grew all his vegetables. Us children grew up with a strong sense of animal husbandry and food production. Skinning a rabbit was normal – I can still picture my granddad teaching me how to do it. On Sundays, my grandmother started cooking lunch in the morning so it would be ready after mass at midday. There was always a roast rabbit, chicken or pigeons. And then there was the ritual of making a clear broth from chicken, veal bones and vegetables that bubbled away slowly and was used for risotto, served as a first course at lunch. The rest was used for a supper of ravioli in a clear broth, boiled meats and fruit mustard or pickles. My mother has kept the tradition and to this day, this is what still happens on a Sunday. We serve our risotto with salsiccia luganega, a local pork sausage that we cook in a pan with a little olive oil and a splash of wine. The original recipe requires the sausage to be cooked with the rice, but we prefer to serve it on top. If you can't find luganega or an Italian-style sausage, the risotto is still delicious on its own without it.

Serves 4

1 litre chicken stock

200g unsalted butter, divided

¼ small onion, finely chopped

350g Carnaroli or Maratelli rice

200ml dry white wine, plush an extra splash for the sausage

3 saffron threads or 1 sachet of saffron powder

a pinch of salt

50g Parmigiano Reggiano cheese, grated

a splash of olive oil

180g salsiccia luganega (or an Italian-style sausage), cut into 5cm pieces

Pour the chicken stock into a saucepan and bring to the boil, then reduce the heat to keep it hot.

Melt 50g of the butter in a heavy-based pan over a medium heat. Add the onion and sweat for just a few minutes, until soft but not coloured. Stir in the rice to coat it in the butter, then pour in the wine and cook until it has all been completely absorbed by the rice.

Add the hot chicken stock one ladleful at a time, stirring until it has all been absorbed before adding another ladle. Stir in the saffron after the first couple of ladles of stock. The rice needs to cook for 15–17 minutes max, so when you get to about 12 minutes, start reducing the amount of stock you're adding in each ladleful, otherwise the risotto may be too wet. The risotto is ready when the grains are soft but still al dente. Season with salt to taste.

Remove the pan from the heat and stir in the remaining 150g butter and the Parmesan cheese. This process is called mantecatura and will give your risotto a silky, creamy texture.

To cook the sausage, heat a splash of olive oil in a separate frying pan over a medium heat. Add the sausage and sauté until it's golden brown all over and cooked through. Add a splash of wine towards the end of the cooking time.

To serve, divide the risotto between four plates and put the sausage on top.

Sausage, chorizo and roast pepper casserole

Mark Anderson, Gather & Gather

When I cook at home, I want a dish that appeals to everyone and is easy to make so that I can be still part of the chats and fun. This recipe changes all the time and is one of the first things I taught my kids, Hannah and Dylan, to cook. They now cook it themselves and have adapted it to be their own versions. Food and cooking are so important in creating relationships and memories and this dish has done that for me repeatedly. It's like a big warm hug on a cold night.

Serves 4

150g orzo

2 tbsp vegetable oil

8 good-quality Irish pork sausages

200g raw cooking chorizo, diced

2 red onions, roughly chopped

1 medium carrot, diced

1 celery stick, finely diced

4 garlic cloves, thinly sliced

2 sprigs of fresh rosemary, needles picked and chopped

1 small bunch of fresh thyme, chopped

1 tsp fennel seeds

salt and freshly ground black pepper

1 tsp hot smoked paprika

50ml sherry vinegar

150ml white wine

500ml chicken stock, divided

500g good-quality passata (I like the Bunalun or Mutti brands)

1 jar of roasted peppers, drained and thinly sliced

1 x 400g tin of cannellini beans, drained and rinsed

½ bunch of fresh flat-leaf parsley, chopped

a few handfuls of rocket, chopped

freshly grated Parmesan, to serve (optional)

Preheat the oven to 200°C (180°C fan).

Cook the orzo in boiling salted water according to the packet instructions, then drain and set aside to cool.

Heat the oil in a large shallow casserole over a medium heat. Add the sausages and brown on all sides. Remove from the casserole and set aside.

Add the diced chorizo to the casserole and cook for 2–3 minutes, until the fat has rendered out and the chorizo is beginning to brown. Add the red onions, carrot, celery, garlic, herbs and fennel seeds and cook for 3–4 minutes, until softened. Season with salt but be careful as the chorizo is often quite salty. Add the smoked paprika and cook for 30 seconds, then deglaze with the sherry vinegar. Once the vinegar has bubbled down and become sticky, pour in the white wine and allow it to reduce by half.

After the wine has reduced, add 350ml of the stock along with the passata, roasted peppers, cannellini beans and cooked orzo. Bring to the boil, then cover with a lid or foil and transfer to the preheated oven.

Cook for 5 minutes, then check the casserole and add the remaining 150ml of stock if it's drying out. Cover and return to the oven to cook for another 5 minutes, at which point the sausages should be completely cooked and the pasta should have warmed through.

To finish, remove from the oven, remove the lid or foil and stir in the chopped parsley and rocket. Drizzle with a little good olive oil and adjust the seasoning with salt and pepper if necessary. Finish with freshly grated Parmesan if you want to add a little luxury.

Lamb

Six Nations stew

Domini Kemp, ITSA food group

Home is your haven; it is your duvet, your shelter. It's where good things come from the kitchen – to nourish, feed and give back to everyone in the home. It's about sitting around the table and having conversations with food that matters.

Lamb is hands-down my favourite meat and there is nothing more comforting than a bowl of mildly spicy stew with a bit of sweet umami in every bite.

Serves 12

100ml olive oil

3kg diced lamb

salt and freshly ground black pepper

6 red onions, thinly sliced

1 head of garlic, cloves peeled and sliced

1 big piece of fresh ginger, peeled and grated

2–3 tbsp harissa

1 tbsp Chinese five-spice powder

1.5 litres stock

4 x 400g tins of chopped tomatoes

4 bay leaves

400g stoned prunes

50ml soy sauce or tamari

50ml maple syrup

To serve:

mashed potatoes or roast sweet potatoes

Heat some of the olive oil in a large frying pan. Working in batches, add the lamb, season it well and cook until browned all over.

Heat the remaining oil in a large heavy-based saucepan or casserole over a medium heat. Add the onions and sweat for about 10 minutes, until soft. Add the garlic, ginger, harissa and five-spice, mix well and cook for another few minutes.

When the lamb is all browned, add it to the onions. Deglaze the frying pan that you cooked the lamb in with some of the stock, making sure to scrape up any crispy browned bits, and pour it all into the onions too. Stir in the tinned tomatoes and bay leaves along with the rest of the stock.

Bring to a boil, then reduce the heat and simmer on the hob for about 1½ hours, stirring occasionally. Alternatively, if you're using a Le Creuset-style casserole, you could cook it in the oven at 160°C (140°C fan), covered with a lid, for 2–3 hours, until the meat is so tender you can cut it with a spoon. Keep the lid on for 1 hour, then remove it so the stew can reduce and thicken up.

When the lamb is done, add the prunes, soy sauce or tamari and the maple syrup. Cook for another 20 minutes, then allow to cool slightly and taste, adjusting the seasoning as necessary.

This is delicious with mash or roast sweet potatoes and tastes great the next day too.

Lamb casserole
with salsa verde

Aidan Mc Grath, Wild Honey Inn

Familiar smells can remind us of home – like a home-cooked dinner, for example. Lamb is the one meat in your butcher shop that is usually from a local farmer. It's also as close to organic meat as you can get without it being labelled as such, especially here in the Burren on the north-west coast of County Clare. You need to use a cheaper cut of meat for this recipe that becomes tender and full of flavour when cooked slowly and gently for a long time in the oven. Choose a cut such as scrag end of lamb (now called neck fillet), which is what I use, or a shoulder would be fine too – something that can withstand the extended cooking time. Ask your butcher to bone it out and tie it for you. This holds the meat together and makes it easier to brown in one or two pieces. It makes carving easier too.

Serves 4

olive oil, for cooking

2 lamb necks, boned and rolled (see the intro)

salt and freshly ground pepper (I use white peppercorns)

2–3 medium onions, finely chopped

8 garlic cloves, peeled and left whole

200–300ml red wine, plus extra

½ dessertspoon tomato purée

500–750ml lamb jus or stock

2 large carrots, each cut into 4 even pieces

2 large parsnips, each cut into 4 even pieces

12 new potatoes, left whole

1 leek, cut into 4 even pieces (optional)

Preheat the oven to 150°C (130°C fan).

Heat some olive oil in a large frying pan over a high heat. Season the lamb with salt only, then add it to the hot oil to seal, making sure you get a good colour on all sides.

At the same time, heat some more oil in a large heavy-based casserole over a medium heat. Add the onions and a pinch of salt and cook for 10 minutes, until softened. Add the garlic and cook for 1 minute more, just until fragrant. Pour in the wine and raise the heat to high to allow it to reduce, then lower the heat, stir in the tomato purée and cook for 1 minute. Transfer the browned lamb to the casserole.

Tie all the bouquet garni ingredients together, then add it to the casserole along with just enough of the jus or stock to cover the lamb. Season with salt and ground white pepper. Bring to a simmer and skim off any scum from the surface, then cover with a lid and cook in the preheated oven for 1½ hours.

Put the carrots and parsnips in the pan that you browned the lamb in and cook for 5–10 minutes, until lightly coloured. Deglaze the pan with a little extra wine, scraping up all the browned bits. Allow it to reduce down, then remove the casserole from the oven and stir in the vegetables. Bring to a simmer on the hob, then return to the oven for 1 hour more, until the meat and vegetables are tender. >>

For the bouquet garni:

2 celery sticks

2 sprigs of fresh thyme

1 sprig of fresh rosemary

1 sprig of fresh curly parsley

1 large bay leaf

For the salsa verde:

2 big handfuls of fresh
flat-leaf parsley

1 bunch of fresh basil

1 bunch of fresh mint

25g capers

6 good-quality anchovy fillets

5 gherkins

2-3 garlic cloves, peeled

8 tbsp really good extra virgin
olive oil

3 tbsp red wine vinegar

1 tbsp Dijon mustard

For the spinach:

a knob of butter

1 very small garlic clove,
finely grated

500g baby spinach

Meanwhile, boil the potatoes until they're cooked through, then peel them while they're still warm.

About 20-30 minutes before the end of the lamb's cooking time, add the potatoes to the casserole along with the leek (if using). Turn down the oven temperature to 120°C (100°C fan) – the dish will finish cooking in the residual heat. The liquid should not boil at any point or the jus will look cloudy and grey from the potatoes, the meat will toughen and the vegetables will overcook. Check the lamb with a roasting fork – if it slips off easily, it's done.

To make the salsa verde, put all the ingredients in a food processor, blend until smooth and season to taste, but remember that the anchovies are salty. Adjust with vinegar and/or olive oil.

To prepare the spinach, melt the butter in a large frying pan over a medium heat. Add the garlic and cook for 1 minute, until fragrant, then add the spinach and cook for 2-3 minutes more, just until it has wilted down. Season with salt and pepper.

Serve the casserole with bowls of the spinach and salsa verde on the side. Add a spoonful of salsa verde on top of each portion.

{tips}

Some summer green veg can also be added at the very end of the cooking time, for example peas, broad beans or French beans. They will cook in the residual heat and add a touch of colour.

You could cook this in a pressure cooker to reduce the cooking time to under an hour (40–50 minutes depending on the meat used), in which case I would keep the meat on the bone. The benefits of using a pressure cooker are that the sealed pot traps all the flavours and aromas inside, it's more energy efficient and it's quicker.

'We have to count our **blessings** when it comes to having a home these days – in some people's eyes, it is nearly a luxury. With life's struggles and challenges, I love to come back to my **home**. I love that feeling of opening my front door, doing a bit of cooking after being out in college or work all day, and closing that door. I feel **safe** and **warm** in my place. But it was not handed to me – with hard work and the help of Peter McVerry Trust, that **opportunity** was given to me, so I continue to work hard to keep my home. With so many people sleeping rough or in hostels, I can't help but feel **grateful** that it's not me anymore.'

Jonathan, Dublin

Spiced lamb shoulder
with bulghur wheat

Ahmet Dede, Dede at the Customs House

This isn't a complicated dish, but it does require a bit of advance planning to allow a full 24 hours for the meat to marinate. It makes a beautiful meal to share with loved ones and it gives me pleasure to make it for them.

Serves 6–8

100ml olive oil

2 onions, thinly sliced

4 garlic cloves, sliced

peel of 1 lemon

6 dried or fresh lime leaves

1 tbsp za'atar spice mix

1 tbsp ground cumin

2 tsp dried chilli flakes

salt and freshly ground black pepper

3 sprigs of fresh mint

1 medium-sized lamb shoulder, deboned (ask your butcher to do this for you)

For the bulghur wheat:

approx. 1 litre chicken stock

100ml olive oil

1 onion, diced

1 red pepper, diced

6 garlic cloves, finely chopped

3 green jalapeños, deseeded and finely diced

2 tbsp red pepper purée or tomato purée

1 tbsp dried mint

Heat a good amount of the oil in a saucepan over a medium heat. Add the onions and cook, stirring occasionally and being careful not to let them burn, for 20 minutes, until they have a nice colour and are lightly caramelised. Add the rest of the olive oil along with the garlic, lemon peel, lime leaves, za'atar, cumin, chilli flakes and ½ teaspoon ground black pepper. Reduce the heat to low and warm gently for 20 minutes – you are not cooking anymore, but rather allowing the flavours to infuse. Remove the pan from the heat and add the mint sprigs, then allow to cool.

Rub the lamb shoulder all over with this spiced oil, then leave it in the fridge for a full 24 hours to marinate.

The next day, preheat the oven to 210°C (190°C fan).

Wrap the lamb shoulder in foil to create a parcel. Make sure there are plenty of layers of foil and that they are all tightly sealed so that the steam stays locked in.

Put the foil-wrapped lamb in a roasting tin, then cook in the preheated oven for 45 minutes. Reduce the temperature to 150°C (130°C fan) and cook for another 1½ hours, then drop the temperature yet again to 110°C (90°C fan) and cook for another 3 hours. Switch off the oven and let the lamb rest – do not open the tin foil until it cools.

Meanwhile, to prepare the bulghur wheat, put the chicken stock in a small saucepan, bring it to a boil and keep it simmering. >>

1 tbsp paprika

1 tsp smoked paprika

1 tsp ground cumin

400g bulghur wheat

1 preserved lemon, finely diced
(or the zest of 1 lemon)

50ml lemon juice

20g fresh flat-leaf parsley,
chopped

20g fresh mint, chopped

150g feta cheese, crumbled

extra virgin olive oil, for drizzling

To serve:

flatbreads (try Graham
Herterich's recipe on page 48)

Heat the oil in a large saucepan on a medium heat. Add the onion, red pepper, garlic and jalapeños along with 1 teaspoon salt. Cook for 10 minutes, until softened, then add the pepper or tomato purée and cook for 2 minutes. Add the dried mint and spices and cook for 1 minute more, then raise the heat to high, stir in the bulghur wheat and toast it for 1 minute.

Pour the boiling stock over the bulghur wheat mixture, making sure there is enough to cover the bulghur with a centimetre or so above to spare. Stir once to level the stock off around the pan, then cover with a lid. Turn the heat down as low as possible and cook for 10 minutes exactly.

After 10 minutes, take the pan off the heat and remove the lid. Put a clean tea towel on top of the saucepan, then put the lid back on. Let this rest for 40 minutes.

To finish, open the lid, remove the tea towel and fluff up the bulghur wheat with a fork. Stir in the preserved lemon or lemon zest, lemon juice and chopped fresh herbs. Taste to check the seasoning, adjusting with salt and pepper as needed. Transfer to a nice serving bowl, sprinkle the crumbled feta on drop and drizzle with extra virgin olive oil.

To serve, open the foil parcel, being careful in case any hot steam escapes. Tip the lamb out into the roasting tin with all the juices from the foil parcel and pull apart into nice chunky pieces. Season to taste, then transfer to a serving platter and bring it to the table with the bulghur wheat. Traditionally, we would also eat this with a yogurt flatbread as a dish made to be shared and enjoyed together.

Home

Bricks and mortar is where some people call a home,

For me it is a sanctuary where I can be alone.

Turn that key and open that door,

It's a place I feel safe and a whole lot more.

Words can't describe the feeling I get,

The places I have come from I certainly won't forget.

A place to sit and reflect on my own,

My home is a safe haven and a comfort zone.

It's a place to build memories with family and friends,

Building a new life so the old one ends.

I'm so grateful for the home that I got,

A place to cook and relax, it's my own little beauty spot.

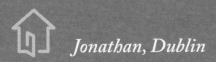

Jonathan, Dublin

Leg of lamb
with nori and seaweed broth

Jp McMahon, Aniar, Cava Bodega, Food on the Edge

Home is a place to cook, share and enjoy time with family and friends. This recipe combines the best of the land and the sea from the West of Ireland.

Serves 8–10

1 leg of lamb, on the bone

light rapeseed oil

sea salt

2 tbsp milled nori

a few sprigs of fresh thyme, leaves picked

2 onions, roughly chopped

2 leeks, roughly chopped

15g dried kelp or kombu

1.5 litres vegetable stock

Preheat the oven to 180°C (160°C fan).

Rub the lamb all over with rapeseed oil and season with salt. Sprinkle the entire lamb leg with the milled nori and thyme.

Spread the onions and leeks on the base of a large roasting tray, then put the lamb on top of the vegetables. Cook in the preheated oven for 1 hour.

Meanwhile, put the dried kelp or kombu in the stock and simmer for 45 minutes.

After 1 hour, pour the seaweed stock into the roasting tray around the lamb. Cook the lamb for another 30–45 minutes, depending on how you like your lamb. After 1½ hours, the lamb should be rare to medium rare and a meat thermometer inserted into the lamb should read between 50°C and 55°C.

Remove the lamb from the oven and allow to rest. Strain the liquid from the tray into a saucepan and bring to a boil, then strain again through a fine mesh sieve.

Carve the lamb and serve in warm bowls with the seaweed broth.

Seafood

Cullen skink

Sally Barnes, Woodcock Smokery

Home to me means safety, comfort, warmth and love. That's how this soup makes me feel on the coldest, wettest of days – and I'm a Scot, so that's really saying something.

Cullen is a fishing village close to Aberdeen in Scotland. Us Scots adore haddock and this recipe uses smoked haddock, which was doubtless prepared in times of plenty. It would have been very salty in the days before refrigeration and vacuum-packing, hence the advice not to add salt to this thick chowder-style soup until the cooking is done and you've had a chance to taste it.

Serves 4

25g butter or extra virgin olive oil

1 large onion, thinly sliced (or see the tips)

2 large floury potatoes, peeled and chopped into bite-sized cubes

500ml milk (or see the tips)

250–300g undyed smoked haddock (or smoked skinless white pollack or smoked hake)

salt and freshly ground black pepper

a handful of fresh parsley, chopped

To serve:

good crusty bread and butter

Melt the butter or oil in a saucepan over a medium heat. Add the onion and gently sauté until translucent but not coloured. Add the potatoes and stir to coat in the flavourful butter or oil, then stir in the milk. Let the soup come up to a simmer – be careful not to let the soup boil or the milk will curdle. Simmer for 15 minutes, until the potatoes are soft.

Meanwhile, skin the smoked fish and remove any bones. Cut the fish into chunks, then stir them into the soup and bring everything back to a simmer. Season with salt and pepper to taste, but the fish already has salt in it, so you may not need more. Cook for 5 minutes more, just until the fish is warmed through.

Garnish with chopped parsley and serve with crusty bread and butter.

{*tips*}

I add two good handfuls of three-cornered leek that I forage from the garden, cleaned and chopped – flowers included – instead of onions when it's in season.

Lactose-intolerant souls can use a freshly prepared white fish stock instead of milk. Boil two fish carcasses (everything except the stomach) with a whole shallot or onion, a few bay leaves and a celery stalk for at least half an hour. Strain through a fine mesh sieve, then use as above to replace the milk.

Smoked haddock risotto

Aishling Moore, Goldie

Home is all about comfort, peace and freedom and I love to cook this recipe at home. It's a one-pot wonder and it reheats well a day later too. Smoked haddock is a great product with a good shelf life, so it's rarely unavailable.

Serves 4

1.2 litres fish stock

olive oil, for cooking

1 onion, diced

1 celery stick, diced

½ leek, diced

salt and ground white and black pepper

3 garlic cloves, finely chopped

65g butter

300g Arborio rice

125ml white wine

250g natural smoked haddock, diced into 1cm pieces

100g frozen peas

1 bunch of fresh flat-leaf parsley, chopped

juice of ½ lemon

Put the fish stock in a saucepan set on a medium heat to keep warm.

Heat a splash of olive oil in a large heavy-based pot over a medium heat. Add the onion, celery and leek and sweat gently for 5–6 minutes, until softened. Season with salt and white pepper, then add the garlic and sweat for 2 minutes more.

Add the butter and allow it to melt, then stir in the rice and cook for 2 minutes, making sure all the grains of rice get coated in the butter. Add the wine and allow it to bubble up to cook off the alcohol, stirring until it has all been absorbed into the rice.

Using a ladle or a measuring jug, add approximately 100ml of the warm stock to the rice at a time, stirring regularly and allowing the rice to absorb all the stock before you add the next 100ml. This will take 20–25 minutes.

Once all the stock has been absorbed by the rice, add the diced smoked haddock and frozen peas and cook for 2 minutes.

Stir in the chopped parsley and lemon juice and season with salt and lots of black pepper. Serve straightaway.

Smoked salmon, chorizo and potato gratin

Ruth Healy, Urru Culinary Store

Home is arriving in to the aroma of baking or cooking and knowing straightaway what is in the oven. It's the freedom to open the fridge, turn on the kettle and pick at whatever is on the counter without asking – like this potato gratin. Potato gratin ticks all the boxes: tasty and nutritious; a flexible one-dish wonder; veggie or meaty; elegant or rustic; penny-pinching or extravagant. The basic recipe consists of potatoes, creamy milk, seasoning and a grated cheese topping. This is my preferred version but use your personal taste, creativity and availability of ingredients to make up your own satisfying gratin based on the basic recipe.

Serves 4

a knob of butter

1 garlic clove, cut in half across the short side

8 medium or large potatoes, peeled and thinly sliced

100g smoked salmon, torn into manageable strips

100g chorizo, sliced

a pinch of grated nutmeg

salt and ground white pepper

500ml milk

200ml cream

200g Cheddar or Gruyère cheese, grated

To serve:

buttered peas

green leafy vegetables or salad

Preheat the oven to 200°C (180°C fan). Butter the base and sides of a 35cm x 20cm dish, then rub it with the cut side of the halved garlic clove.

Soak the potato slices in cold water until ready to use, then drain and pat dry in a clean tea towel (or see the tips). Start with an overlapping layer of potatoes in the bottom of the dish, then add a layer of the smoked salmon, more potatoes, a layer of chorizo and finish with a layer of potatoes. Sprinkle a little nutmeg, salt and white pepper on each layer as you go.

Stir the milk and cream together and pour it over the potatoes. Sprinkle the grated cheese on top. Bake in the preheated oven for 45 minutes, until the potatoes are soft and creamy.

Serve with buttered peas and green leafy vegetables or a salad.

{*tips*}

*In a rush? Bring the potato slices, milk and cream to a gentle simmer in a saucepan. Cook for 5 minutes.
Use one-third for each layer.*

For a veggie option, replace the salmon and chorizo with leeks, mushrooms and thyme.

*For a richer version, increase the cream and reduce the milk.
Add a sprinkle of grated cheese to each layer.*

For a lighter version, replace the cream with stock.

Sweet and sour fish curry

Sunil Ghai, Pickle, Tiffin and Street

Home means everything to me, whether it's my home here in Ireland or in India. Home is where you share your sorrows, stress and happiness. Home brings strength and togetherness. Home means food cooked by or for your loved ones.

I learned this recipe from my colleague's mother, who used to cook this all the time for us. I am actually not very fond of seafood, but when we visited my friend, his mother cooked this. I only tasted the sauce and fell in love with the curry. It's very simple but it's all about technique: when to add the spice or tomato or chilli and knowing how much to use. I have simplified the recipe a bit so that everyone can fall in love with it, just like I did.

Serves 4

vegetable oil, for cooking

150g red onion, finely diced

10 curry leaves

½ tsp fenugreek seeds

20g fresh ginger, finely chopped

2 garlic cloves, finely chopped

½ tbsp Kashmiri chilli powder or paprika

1 tsp ground coriander

1 dried red chilli, torn in half

½ tsp ground turmeric

½ tsp fenugreek seed powder

1½ tbsp tomato purée

60–80ml coconut milk

4 sea bass fillets, cut into large chunks

sea salt

1–2 tsp lime juice

1–2 tbsp roughly chopped fresh coriander, plus extra to garnish

honey or brown sugar, to taste

Heat a generous drizzle of oil in a large, deep pan set over a medium-high heat. Once the oil has reached the smoking point, add the red onion, curry leaves and fenugreek seeds. Reduce the heat to medium-low and cook for about 10 minutes, until the onions are golden brown.

Reduce the heat to low, stir in the ginger and garlic and cook for 1–2 minutes, just until fragrant. Add the chilli powder or paprika and the ground coriander along with a small splash of water. Cook, stirring, for 1–2 minutes. Stir in the dried red chilli, turmeric and fenugreek seed powder, then mix in the tomato purée with another generous splash of water.

Stir in just enough coconut milk to make a thin sauce, then add the fish, making sure it's covered in sauce. Season with a generous pinch of salt and simmer for 15 minutes.

Just before serving, stir in the lime juice and fresh coriander. Finally, stir in a little honey or brown sugar to taste to add a little sweetness to the curry. Garnish with a little more fresh coriander and serve hot.

Turbot
with potato wedges and coriander and chilli salsa

Tara Walker, chef

This is my family's go-to recipe when we've been having a busy time or just need a nice dinner together. I have been making this for about 20 years and although it is a treat since turbot, brill and John Dory can be expensive, the actual cooking and preparation are fairly minimal. This is where the beautiful fresh fish we have available to us really shines with minimum intervention from the cook.

Serves 2

plain flour, enough to coat the fish

2 fillets of turbot, brill or John Dory

1 tbsp butter, softened

For the coriander and chilli salsa:

1 bunch of fresh coriander, chopped

1 garlic clove, finely chopped

1 fresh red chilli, deseeded and finely chopped

2 tbsp olive oil

juice of 1 lemon

salt and freshly ground black pepper

For the potato wedges:

2 potatoes, scrubbed and cut into wedges

rapeseed oil, for roasting

½ tsp onion salt

½ tsp garlic granules

1 sprig of fresh rosemary, chopped

To serve:

green vegetables or a baby leaf salad

Preheat the oven to 200°C (180°C fan).

First make the salsa. Put the coriander, garlic, chilli, olive oil, a squeeze of lemon juice and some salt and pepper in a small bowl. Taste for seasoning, adjusting the lemon or salt if necessary. Set aside to let the flavours marry together.

To make the wedges, put the potatoes in an ovenproof dish and drizzle with a little rapeseed oil. Sprinkle the onion salt, garlic granules and rosemary over them, then shake them about to coat evenly. Roast in the preheated oven for 25–35 minutes, shaking the dish every now and then to make sure they cook evenly.

To cook the fish, put a little plain flour on a plate and season with salt and pepper. Pat the fish dry with kitchen paper or a clean tea towel, then dredge it in the flour to coat, shaking off any excess. Spread the butter on the fish as if you were buttering a piece of bread.

Heat a dry frying pan on the hob until it's very hot, almost smoking. Put the fish in the pan, flesh side down – it should sizzle. When the fish domes, turn it and cook for a couple minutes on the skin side. Remove to a warm plate and drizzle with the coriander and chilli salsa.

Serve with the oven-roasted potato wedges and green vegetables or a baby leaf salad.

Mediterranean seafood casserole
with chorizo and chickpeas

Niall Sabongi, Sustainable Seafood Ireland

This is my go-to dish to cook at home for the people I love most. I like to use line-caught pollock – it's local, sustainable and delicious – and red mullet, which gives it a Mediterranean feel. But you can use any fish you like, such as hake, brill, cod, turbot or even shellfish.

Serves 2–4

For the roast vegetables:

2 large potatoes, cut into slices 1cm thick

1 onion, cut into slices 1cm thick

1 red pepper, cut into slices 1cm thick

1 lemon, sliced as thinly as you can

1 garlic clove, grated or crushed

salt and freshly ground black pepper

For the casserole:

6 tbsp olive oil, plus extra

½ raw chorizo sausage, diced

1 onion, diced

5 garlic cloves, sliced

1 tbsp paprika

½ tbsp chilli powder

½ tbsp ground cumin

½ tbsp coriander seeds, crushed

½ tbsp caraway seeds

a few strands of saffron

600ml warm water

2 tbsp tomato purée

1 x 400g tin of chickpeas, drained and rinsed

200g fish per person (see the intro)

To serve:

good crusty bread

Preheat the oven to 240°C (conventional or fan) or as high as it will go.

Toss the sliced potatoes, onion, pepper and lemon with the garlic, a splash of olive oil and some salt and pepper on a baking tray. Roast in the preheated oven for 15 minutes. Set aside.

Reduce the oven temperature to 220°C (200°C fan).

Heat the 6 tablespoons of oil in a large heavy-based casserole over a medium-low heat. Add the chorizo and cook for 3–4 minutes. Add the onion and cook for 3 minutes, then add the garlic and cook for 2 minutes more. Add the paprika, chilli powder, cumin, coriander and caraway seeds and cook gently for 1–2 minutes.

Put the saffron in a measuring jug with the warm water, tomato purée, 1 tablespoon salt and a good twist of pepper. Allow to sit for 5 minutes, then add this to the casserole along with the chickpeas. Simmer for 4–5 minutes and taste for seasoning.

Add the roasted vegetables along with all their juices from the baking tray, then nestle in the fish and drizzle with 2–3 tablespoons of olive oil. Transfer the casserole to the oven and cook for 15 minutes, until the fish is cooked through. Allow to rest for 5 minutes.

Serve straight to the table with crusty bread for mopping it all up.

Vegetarian

Salad of summer fruit and goat cheese

Siobhán Ní Ghairbhith, St Tola

Home means having conversations about what's important in life, sharing memories together and spending quality time with my family in our garden or house.

This is my go-to recipe during the summer, which I serve with boiled new potatoes with lashings of butter and fresh herbs. It was shared with me by a chef colleague of mine, Maura Foley from Shelbourne Lodge in Kenmare.

Serves 4

250g fresh strawberries, quartered or halved (or left whole if they are very small)

100g fresh raspberries

2 ripe nectarines, sliced

4 handfuls of mixed baby salad leaves

1 tbsp chopped fresh oregano or basil leaves

4 tbsp St Tola soft goat cheese

2 tbsp flaked almonds, toasted

For the citrus dressing:

3 tbsp fresh orange juice

1 tbsp fresh lemon juice

1 tbsp honey, warmed to help it combine

6 tbsp extra virgin olive oil

salt and freshly ground black pepper

To make the dressing, pour the orange and lemon juice and the warm honey in a jar with a tight-fitting lid. Shake to combine, then add the oil and seasoning and shake again to mix. Taste and adjust the seasoning if needed.

Put the strawberries, raspberries and nectarines in a large bowl with 2 tablespoons of the dressing and toss gently to coat. Put the salad leaves and fresh herbs in a separate bowl with another 2 tablespoons of dressing and toss to coat.

To serve, divide the dressed salad leaves between four plates, then scatter over the fruit, goat cheese and almonds. Serve the remaining dressing on the side for anyone who would like to add a little more.

Roasted carrots
with spicy blood orange honey, hazelnuts and goat cheese

Jack and Theo Kirwan, Sprout & Co.

Cooking at home should be simple, adaptable and full of flavour. We've used carrots but that could easily change throughout the year – think beets, Hispi cabbage or courgettes. But the infused honey is the star. This liquid gold can be your secret weapon in the kitchen. Drizzle it over yogurt, use it in a salad dressing or spread it over toast.

Serves 4

1 bunch of baby carrots, peeled and halved lengthways

1 tbsp olive oil, plus extra for brushing

salt and freshly ground black pepper

100g hazelnuts, skin on

150g soft Irish goat cheese, crumbled

For the blood orange honey:

1 blood orange, zested and halved

2 fresh red chillies, skin pierced with a sharp knife

300ml honey

2 sprigs of fresh rosemary

To garnish:

1–2 spring onions, thinly sliced

a few sprigs of fresh coriander, leaves picked

To make the honey, put a ridged chargrill pan over a high heat. Brush the chillies and the blood orange halves lightly with olive oil. Put the chillies on the hot pan and cook for about 4 minutes on each side, until blackened. Put the oranges on the pan at the same time, cut side down, and cook for 5 minutes, until charred. Pour the honey into a saucepan, then add the charred oranges, cut side down, along with the blackened chillies and the rosemary. Bring to a simmer, then take the pan off the heat and set aside to infuse and cool.

Squeeze all the juice from the oranges into the honey and set aside the gooey sweet chillies to use later on top of the salad. Strain the honey into a jar with a sealed lid.

Preheat the oven to 200°C.

Put the carrots on a baking tray, drizzle with the olive oil and season with salt and pepper. Roast in the preheated oven for 15 minutes.

At the same time, put the hazelnuts on a baking tray and toast in the oven for 8–10 minutes, until golden brown. Put them in the middle of a clean tea towel, then gather up the edges and rub them with the towel to remove their skins. Lightly crush the nuts with a knife or in a pestle and mortar, then tip into a bowl. Sprinkle the goat cheese over the hazelnuts along with the orange zest.

To serve, transfer the roasted carrots to a large serving platter and spoon clusters of goat cheese and hazelnuts around them. Drizzle the honey over everything. Chop the gooey chillies and scatter them over along with the spring onions and coriander leaves, some flaky sea salt and a drizzle of olive oil.

Kale, tomato and Parmesan soup

Caitlin Ruth, Caitlin Ruth Food

Anyone who has experienced housing insecurity can tell you that the feeling of relief that comes from having a safe place to retreat to is the best feeling in the whole world. After 25 years living in the same tiny house, I thank my lucky stars every time I open my front door.

Starting in mid to late August, our local growers have an abundance of kale, courgettes and tomatoes. This hearty soup uses all three and gives purpose to the Parmesan rinds I save in a bag in the freezer. We never get tired of this soup.

Serves 6

100ml extra virgin olive oil

250g diced onion

250g diced carrot

200g thinly sliced celery

a few pinches of dried chilli flakes or chopped fresh chillies

a big pinch of fennel seeds

3 medium courgettes, sliced

500g kale (my favourite is Tuscan kale)

600g ripe tomatoes, roughly chopped

3 garlic cloves, peeled

1 fresh rosemary sprig, leaves stripped

75–150g Parmesan rinds (the more rinds, the more flavour!)

salt and freshly ground black pepper

Heat the olive oil in a large soup pot over a medium heat. Add the onion, carrot, celery, chilli and fennel seeds and cook for about 10 minutes, until the veg are softened and the onion is translucent. Add the courgettes and cook for a further 5 minutes.

Meanwhile, bring a pot of salted water to the boil. Strip the kale off the stalks, then plunge the leaves into the boiling water and cook for 5 minutes. Drain and refresh under cold running water. Squeeze all the water out of the kale and chop it finely. Set aside.

Put the tomatoes in a large jug along with the garlic, rosemary and half of the cooked kale. Add 1 litre of cold water, then blend with a hand-held blender until nearly smooth. Pour this tomato mix on top of the cooked veg in the soup pot. Add the Parmesan rinds and 1 more litre of water and simmer for 1 hour. Add the rest of the chopped cooked kale and simmer for another 20 minutes. Add plenty of salt and pepper to taste – this soup needs a lot of salt!

You can eat this straightaway, but it's even better the next day. Refrigerate it with the Parmesan rinds still in the soup – they keep adding flavour – but fish them out and discard them before serving.

Dillisk, leek and Cheddar tart

John and Sally McKenna, McKennas' Guides

Our job takes us all over Ireland, tasting food in many wonderful restaurants. Ironically, this makes us appreciate home cooking even more. We especially enjoy being able to say, well, we're home for two weeks now, so it's time to bake bread or make pastry. We know we're really at home when we're making this tart, sometimes (not always) taking time to pick the dillisk from the local beach, where it grows on the washed-up strips of brown kelp.

Serves 6

For the pastry:

160g plain flour

1 tsp salt

60g cold butter, cut into cubes

2 tbsp plus 1 tsp cold water

For the filling:

50g butter

3 medium-sized leeks

50ml water

salt and freshly ground black pepper

a handful of roughly chopped fresh dillisk

2 eggs

100g grated Cheddar cheese

250ml cream

1 tbsp Dijon mustard

To make the pastry, put the flour and salt in a large bowl. Add the cold butter and rub it into the flour with your fingers. Add the cold water drop by drop, mixing just until everything comes together into a ball. Cover with a butter wrapper or wrap in cling film and refrigerate for 1 hour, until chilled.

Roll out the chilled pastry to line a 20cm flan dish. Put the butter wrapper or cling film on top of the pastry and place the pastry-lined dish in the freezer for another couple of hours, until it's hard and frozen. (If you want to keep it in the freezer for longer, then completely wrap it in cling film first to protect it.)

Preheat the oven to 200°C (180°C fan).

Prick the base of the pastry all over with a fork, then pre-bake the pastry in the preheated oven for about 20 minutes, until golden. There is no need to use baking beans if using this frozen dough.

To make the filling, melt the butter in a saucepan over a medium heat. Add the leeks and sauté for about 5 minutes, until they start to soften. Add the water and season with salt. Cover and cook for a further 5 minutes. Season again, this time with black pepper and the roughly chopped dillisk. Remove the pan from the heat and allow to cool slightly.

Beat the eggs in a bowl and stir in the grated cheese, cream and mustard, then fold in the cooled leeks. Pour this custard into the part-cooked pastry shell and bake in the oven for approximately 20 minutes, until the filling is just firm. Cut into wedges to serve.

Mac 'n' cheese

Jess Murphy, Kai

Every time my mum comes to visit me in Galway from New Zealand, mac 'n' cheese is the one thing I always ask her to make for me. It's nurturing, wholesome and can feed a crowd. You might have to use every pot in the house, but that just extends your time and chats with your loved one.

Serves 8–10

400g macaroni

50g butter

1 medium onion, chopped

4 garlic cloves, crushed

4 tinned anchovies

200ml Gavi white wine

50g plain flour

1.2 litres full-fat milk

2 tsp mustard powder

a large pinch of cayenne pepper

120g Kylemore cheese, grated

120g smoked Gubbeen cheese, grated

2 balls of scamorza cheese (important for the cheese stretch!), chopped

a pinch of freshly grated nutmeg

To serve:

garlic bread

watercress salad

Preheat the oven to 205°C (185°C fan).

Cook the pasta in a pot of boiling salted water according to the packet instructions. Drain and set aside.

Melt the butter in a large heavy-based pot over a medium heat. Add the onion and cook for about 10 minutes, until soft, then add the garlic and anchovies and cook for 1–2 minutes more, until the anchovies start to break down.

Turn the heat up and add the white wine. Let it reduce down, then add the flour, milk, mustard and cayenne, stirring until it's a lovely, super-thick sauce.

Stir the cooked pasta, most of the cheeses and a pinch of grated nutmeg into the sauce, then transfer it all to a big baking dish and scatter over the rest of the cheese.

Bake on the lower rack of the preheated oven for around 20 minutes, until golden brown and crisp on top – we want bubbling, melting heaven.

Serve to a round of applause from your mates and family with shop-bought garlic bread and a peppery watercress salad.

Wild garlic mashotto
with sprouting broccoli and beluga lentils

Denis Cotter, Paradiso

Mash is my comfort food. On a fragile couch day, it might be just plain buttery mash with no more than a dusting of grated sheep's cheese. One of my cookbooks, *For the Love of Food*, has a whole chapter of variations on mash, presented as a plea to have mash and the potato itself treated with the reverence given to risotto and rice – which, after all, is no more than the Italian equivalent of a bowl of mash. I hereby resurrect the campaign for mashotto – mash as risotto!

Serves 4

For the lentils:

30g beluga lentils

50ml olive oil

2 shallots, finely chopped

10 sungold tomatoes, halved

zest of 1 orange

zest of 1 lemon

salt and freshly ground black pepper

For the wild garlic mash:

1.2kg floury potatoes, peeled and chopped

100g butter

150ml milk

a small handful of wild garlic leaves, finely chopped

For the broccoli:

2 tbsp olive oil

1 red onion, halved and thinly sliced

2 handfuls of sprouting broccoli stalks

2 fresh red chillies, deseeded and thinly sliced

To finish:

50g hard sheep's cheese, such as Cratloe Hills or Cáis na Tíre, finely grated

Cook the lentils in plenty of boiling water for about 20 minutes, until just done. Drain and rinse briefly to cool, then set aside.

Heat 2 tablespoons of the olive oil in a pan over a medium heat. Add the shallots and sauté for 2 minutes. Add the sungolds and cook for a minute to soften, then add the cooked lentils, the orange and lemon zest and the remaining olive oil. Season well with salt, then remove the pan from the heat and set aside.

Meanwhile, boil or steam the potatoes until cooked through. Warm the butter, milk and wild garlic in a large pan. Add the cooked potatoes and mash gently to get a smooth but firm purée. You can also do this by passing the cooked potatoes through a ricer and stirring this into the warmed milk and butter. Season with salt and pepper.

At the same time, to prepare the broccoli, heat the 2 tablespoons of olive oil in a wide pan or wok over a high heat. Add the red onion and cook for 1 minute, then add the broccoli and chillies and continue to cook, stirring or tossing often, until the broccoli has browned a little and is tender. Add a splash of water now and then to prevent the broccoli from burning and to partially steam the greens. Season with salt.

To serve, add a little water to the lentils and bring them back to a boil. Use a spatula to spoon mounds of the wild garlic mash into shallow bowls. Add some sprouting broccoli and spoon the lentils over the broccoli, using the juices to form an oily pool of gravy around the mash. Finish with a dusting of finely grated cheese.

Ugly-delicious tomato tart

Claire and Christopher Arnold, Lennox Street Grocer

We come from a background in hospitality: kitchen, front of house, bartending, food tour guide and wine sales. We also come from a large family and were brought up with incredible homemade food. Whether it's in our little Portobello shop or hosting at home, we always like to share foods that we love and this recipe is a great example of that. It's a family favourite that always impresses, but it's really quite simple. It's not the most beautiful tart, but it is incredibly delicious. The short crumbly pastry, sweet tomatoes and tart tomato purée combined with the sweet cheese, fresh herbs and tangy mustard results in a flavour bomb with many dimensions.

Serves 8

1 sheet of shop-bought ready-rolled shortcrust pastry, thawed if frozen

5–6 ripe tomatoes (about 600g)

1½ tbsp Dijon mustard

250g grated Gruyère cheese (Templegall is a special treat)

200g tomato purée

2 tbsp olive oil

100g fresh oregano, finely chopped

100g fresh parsley, finely chopped

salt and freshly ground black pepper

{*tip*}

Fresh oregano can be hard to find in Dublin, but Evergreen on Wexford Street usually has some and big bags of parsley too. If you can't get oregano, though, just double up on the parsley and add some thyme – this recipe doesn't have to be precise to be delicious.

Preheat the oven to 200°C (180°C fan).

Use the ready-rolled pastry to line a 28cm diameter loose-bottomed tart tin. Prick the base all over with a fork, then line the pastry with non-stick baking paper and pour in a layer of dried beans or rice to weight it down. Bake in the preheated oven for 10–15 minutes, until the pastry is firm. Remove the paper and beans or rice, then return to the oven to bake for 5 minutes more, until golden. Set aside to cool slightly on a wire rack.

Meanwhile, cut the tomatoes into slices 1cm thick, then lay them on a piece of kitchen paper in a single layer and pat them dry with more paper. This helps prevent the tart getting soggy.

Spread the cooked pastry case with the Dijon mustard and sprinkle with a layer of grated cheese. Arrange the sliced tomatoes to fill the tart in one layer.

Mix the tomato purée with the oil, herbs, salt and pepper to taste and the remaining grated cheese. Taste and adjust the seasoning, then spread this mix over the tomatoes.

Bake the tart in the preheated oven for 25–30 minutes, until there are one or two spots starting to slightly char or blacken. Let the tart sit until it's close to room temperature – it's perfect cold the next day too.

Garnish with a few fresh oregano or parsley leaves, then cut into wedges to serve.

Dessert

Baked rice pudding

JR Ryall, Ballymaloe House

It's hard to beat a baked rice pudding. I often make it at home as a weeknight treat and serve it with softly whipped cream, a sprinkle of soft dark brown sugar and whatever homemade jam I have on hand. While some cooks claim the best rice puddings are cooked in a pan on the stovetop, my own preference is to bake it slowly in a dish. As it bakes the small amount of rice gradually swells and thickens the milk, which itself reduces in volume as the pudding cooks – herein lies the magic of rice pudding. The rice in the finished dish should be soft and tender, not mushy, and the milk creamy and soothing beneath a light golden top.

Serves 4

100g short grain pudding rice

40g caster sugar

a pinch of salt

a small knob of butter

900ml full-fat milk

To serve:

softly whipped cream

dark brown sugar

good-quality jam (strawberry or raspberry is best)

Preheat the oven to 180°C (160°C fan).

Put the rice, sugar, a pinch of salt and butter into a 1.2-litre capacity pie dish. Bring the milk to a boil and pour it over the rice, stirring gently. Position the dish on a baking sheet in the centre of the preheated oven and bake for 1–1½ hours. The pudding is ready when the skin on top is golden and the rice underneath is cooked through – it should have soaked up the milk but still be soft and creamy.

Serve the pudding warm from the oven with softly whipped cream, a sprinkle of soft dark brown sugar and a spoonful of jam on top.

{*tip*}

Rice pudding can easily be flavoured. Try adding half a vanilla pod split along its length or a few drops of pure vanilla extract along with the rice at the beginning of the method. A pinch of freshly grated nutmeg is also very nice.

Raspberry and rose Victoria sponge cake

Aoife Noonan, pastry chef

Tea in our house always meant cake. It started with my grandparents on my mum's side. Visiting their house was always a fancy affair to me growing up, the table always chock-a-block with lunch bits, pots of strong tea, biscuits and homemade cakes. Victoria sponge is the simplest cake to make and my absolute favourite. The subtle floral notes of rose enhance the sweet raspberries to create a perfect cake for any family occasion.

Serves 8–10

For the sponge:

335g unsalted butter, softened

335g caster sugar

6 large eggs

335g self-raising flour

For the rose and vanilla cream:

600ml cream

35g caster sugar

2 vanilla pods, split in half lengthways and seeds scraped out

200g natural yogurt

1 tsp rosewater

For the raspberry layer:

100g raspberry conserve

125g fresh raspberries

To decorate:

200g fresh raspberries

dried, fresh or crystallised rose petals

icing sugar, for dusting (optional)

Preheat the oven to 180°C (160°C fan). Grease and line 3 x 20cm loose-bottomed sandwich tins with non-stick baking paper.

Cream together the butter and sugar for 2–3 minutes in a stand mixer fitted with the beater attachment until pale and creamy. Add the eggs one by one, beating in each one until fully combined before adding the next. Sift in the flour, mixing until just combined but taking care not to overmix.

Divide the batter between the three tins and bake in the preheated oven for 20–25 minutes, until a skewer inserted into the centre comes out clean. Remove the tins from the oven and leave the sponges to cool slightly before turning out onto a wire rack to cool completely.

To make the rose and vanilla cream, whisk the cream in a large mixing bowl with the sugar and vanilla seeds to soft peaks. Fold the whipped cream into the yogurt and add the rosewater to taste, folding gently to combine. Chill until ready to assemble the cake.

To assemble, trim the cakes to ensure they are all even. Spread the jam evenly on top of two of the sponges. Arrange a few raspberries on top and spread or pipe one-third of the rose and vanilla whipped cream onto the sponge. Place the second jam-covered sponge on top. Repeat with a few more raspberries as before, spreading or piping another third of the cream around them. Place the last sponge on top and finish with the remaining cream. Decorate with the remaining 200g of raspberries and rose petals, then dust with icing sugar (if using). Cut into slices to serve.

Granny Campbell's retro sherry trifle

Georgina Campbell, Georgina Campbell's Ireland Guides

While many recipes become part of a family's best-loved repertoire, very few have followed ours down the generations as persistently as my mother's traditional trifle, which is an absolute must at every Christmas gathering. Served in an old cut-glass bowl dating back to who-knows-when and presented retro-style with blanched split almonds and glacé cherry flowers with angelica leaves, it never fails to raise a smile – and I always make two or there would be no leftovers to enjoy the next day.

Serves 6–8

1 small shop-bought sponge cake or premium-quality trifle sponges

raspberry jam, preferably homemade

150ml approx. sherry, preferably medium or sweet

450g fruit, e.g. poached pears

1 jar of cocktail cherries, drained

300ml cream

For the custard:

425ml creamy milk

1 vanilla pod or a few drops of vanilla extract

3 eggs

25g caster sugar

To decorate (optional):

blanched almonds, glacé cherries and angelica

OR

toasted flaked almonds

To make the custard, put the milk in a pan with the vanilla pod (if using) and bring almost to a boil. Take the pan off the heat, then remove the vanilla pod. You can wash the vanilla pod and pat it dry to reuse.

Whisk the eggs and sugar together lightly in a separate bowl. Gradually whisk the hot milk into the egg mixture. Rinse the pan out with cold water, return the mixture to it and stir over a low heat until it thickens enough to coat the back of a wooden spoon. Do not allow it to boil. Pour the custard into a mixing bowl and set aside, stirring occasionally to prevent a skin forming. If using vanilla extract, stir it in now.

Halve the sponge cake horizontally and spread with raspberry jam to make a sandwich. Cut into slices and use to line the bottom and the lower sides of a large glass trifle dish. Drizzle generously with the sherry. Slice the fruit if necessary, then spread it out over the sponge and intersperse with cocktail cherries tucked in around the fruit to make an even layer. Pour the custard on top, cover with a plate and leave to cool and thicken in the fridge.

Before serving, whip the cream and spread it over the custard, then decorate with the traditional blanched split almonds and the glacé cherry and angelica 'flowers' – or, more simply, with a casual scattering of toasted flaked almonds if you like.

Warm chocolate pudding
with vanilla ice cream

Kevin Burke, Library Street

Dessert is the best part of every meal I have with my friends and family. For some people it's all about the main while others go crazy for little bites, but not me. I live and breathe for sweets and none more so than this chocolate pudding and ice cream. I honestly cannot get enough. If you're not quick enough, I will have it all devoured in seconds. This warm chocolate pudding ticks all the boxes for me: über-rich and chocolatey, served with delicious vanilla ice cream and a splash of Baileys over the top, because why not?

Serves 12

345g butter, diced

330g dark chocolate (at least 70% cocoa solids), roughly chopped

For the sabayon:

150g egg yolks

90g caster sugar

45g honey

40g cornflour

For the meringue:

250g egg whites

125g caster sugar

To serve:

good-quality vanilla ice cream

a splash of Baileys

Put the butter and chocolate in a large heatproof bowl set over a pan of gently simmering water (a bain-marie), making sure the water doesn't touch the bottom of the bowl. Allow to melt, stirring now and then, then remove from the heat and allow to cool slightly.

Put the egg yolks, 90g sugar, honey and cornflour in a large bowl and whisk to form a thickened sabayon.

Separately, whisk the egg whites and the 125g sugar in the clean, dry bowl of a stand mixer fitted with the whisk attachment to form a meringue.

Fold the sabayon into the cooled chocolate mix until fully combined, then carefully fold in the meringue. Pipe 100g of the pudding mix into 12 ramekins and put in the fridge to set (this can be done the night before).

Preheat the oven to 220°C (200°C fan).

Put all the ramekins on two baking trays, then bake the puddings in the preheated oven for 10–12 minutes, until just set but still with a little wobble in the centre. Remove from the oven and allow to stand for 1 minute.

Serve with a scoop of vanilla ice cream and a splash of Baileys over the top.

New York cheesecake

Tara Gartlan, pastry chef

This is my mum's favourite thing in the whole world – she would eat this for breakfast, lunch and dinner. My parents immigrated to New York as teenagers, where my mum discovered baked cheesecake, aka New York cheesecake. It was love at first bite. I make this cheesecake for every family gathering, Mother's Day, Mum's birthday and Christmas Day. I often make it with gluten-free digestives and flour and sometimes make it without the fruit topping or I use a different fruit, but it remains the cake that brings me comfort.

Serves 8–10

For the base:

250g digestive biscuits (I use gluten-free digestive biscuits)

60g salted butter

40g honey

For the cheesecake:

700g full-fat cream cheese

225g caster sugar

2 medium eggs

1 egg yolk

350g cream (I weigh my cream – it's a pastry chef thing!)

2 tsp vanilla essence

40g plain flour (I use gluten-free plain flour), sifted

For the topping:

300g frozen raspberries, thawed

2 tbsp lime marmalade (I use Roe's)

zest of 1 lemon and juice of ½

150g fresh strawberries

Crush the biscuits to fine crumbs in a food processor or with a rolling pin, then put in a mixing bowl. Melt the butter and honey together, then mix into the biscuit crumb. Scrape into the base of a 20cm springform tin and pack down firmly, using the back of a spoon to level it out. Put in the freezer for 20 minutes.

Preheat the oven to 170°C (150°C fan).

Blend the cream cheese and sugar in a food processor until smooth. Scrape down the sides of the bowl, then add the eggs, egg yolk, cream and vanilla. Blend again until smooth, ensuring the eggs are mixed in evenly. Fold in the sifted flour with a spatula or metal spoon.

Pour the cheesecake mix onto the biscuit base. Bake in the preheated oven for 1 hour 10 minutes, until puffy and golden around the edges. It should still have a slight wobble in the centre.

Let the cheesecake cool for 1 hour at room temperature, then chill the cheesecake overnight or for a minimum of 6 hours.

The next day, go around the edge of the tin with a knife to loosen it, then release the cake from the tin.

To make the fruit topping, put half of the raspberries in a small saucepan with the marmalade and the lemon zest and juice. Bring to a boil, then cook for 5 minutes, until the sauce becomes thick and glossy. Pass through a fine mesh sieve to get a smooth sauce, then put this in the fridge for 10 minutes to cool. Discard the pulp left in the sieve. Once the sauce is cool, use it to coat the remaining raspberries and the strawberries, then spoon the fruit on top of the cheesecake.

This will keep for up to five days in the fridge, but it's best enjoyed the day after baking.

Sticky coffee pudding

Russell Alford and Patrick Hanlon, GastroGays

No, that's not a typo, you read it correctly: sticky *coffee* pudding. We all love a sticky toffee pudd but this is a deeper, more indulgent twist on the classic. The espresso powder adds a hum of coffee while the Camp essence adds treacle-like richness. This sauced pudding is made using little bits of ingredients you might already have in your kitchen, so it's a great recipe to have up your sleeve when the desire for a rich pudding strikes – and in our house, that's often.

Serves 6–9

For the sponge:

75g unsalted butter, softened

50g dark brown sugar

2 tbsp Camp Coffee

2 large eggs

150ml full-fat or plant milk

1 tbsp instant espresso powder

150g plain flour

2 tsp baking powder

For the sauce:

200g dark brown sugar

100g butter

1 tbsp Camp Coffee

200ml double cream

To serve:

cream, custard or ice cream

Preheat the oven to 200°C (180°C fan). Grease a rectangular (roughly 25cm x 20cm x 5cm) or square baking dish.

If using a stand mixer, we find it's better to use the whisk attachment here. Put the butter in the bowl and start to mix on a low to medium setting until lightly creamed, then add the sugar and Camp and keep creaming until fluffy. Crack in an egg and mix until totally incorporated before adding the next one and repeating.

Measure your milk in a jug and add the espresso powder, mixing to dissolve. Pour this into the creamed butter, sugar and eggs and mix to combine. Finally, add the flour and baking powder and mix just until it comes together into a thick, smooth batter. Be sure to scrape down the sides to nab any truant specs of flour or other ingredients.

Using a rubber spatula, scrape the batter into the greased baking dish. Give it a shake to even it out, then bake in the centre of the preheated oven for 25–30 minutes, until risen and spongy and a skewer inserted just about comes out clean.

While that bakes, make the sauce. Put the brown sugar, butter and Camp in a heavy-based saucepan on a medium-low heat. Allow everything to melt slowly, coaxing it along by shaking the pan now and then and letting it bubble down and thicken. All in all, it should take 7–10 minutes. Take the pan off the heat and whisk in the double cream.

When the sponge is ready and out of the oven, prick holes all over the sponge with a thin skewer or cocktail stick. Pour over about two-thirds of your sauce (the sizzle of the sauce hitting the sides of the baking dish will have you weak at the knees). Leave it, if you can, for about 25 minutes to cool and absorb the sauce. Pour over the final third of the sauce when serving.

Serve with cream, custard or ice cream – or all three if you fancy.

Peanut butter financiers

Gráinne Mullins, Grá Chocolates

I made my first batch of financiers when I was a little girl after trying them on holiday in France. Financiers are a classic bite-sized browned butter almond tea cake that you often find in French patisseries, but they are made with just a few simple ingredients. Delicate, buttery and full of nutty flavour, they make the perfect dessert or snack served alongside a morning coffee or afternoon tea.

Makes 24

190g ground almonds

300g butter

375g caster sugar

150g plain flour

250g egg whites (approx. 7 eggs)

250g peanut butter

Preheat the oven to 170°C (150°C fan) for 20 minutes.

Spread the ground almonds evenly on a baking sheet and bake in the preheated for about 7 minutes, until pale golden brown. Allow to cool completely.

To make your brown butter (beurre noisette), melt the butter in a small saucepan over a low heat. Continue cooking, stirring constantly and watching carefully to prevent burning, until the milk solids turn deep brown. Immediately pour the butter into a heatproof bowl. Set aside to cool slightly or reheat the beurre noisette when you're ready to add it to the batter.

Sift the flour into a large bowl, then stir in the sugar and toasted ground almonds.

Beat the egg whites in the bowl of a stand mixer fitted with the whisk attachment just until foamy. Add the sugar and flour mixture and beat on a low speed until incorporated. Drizzle in the warm beurre noisette on a medium-low speed for 5 minutes, until it becomes a smooth, golden cream. Add the peanut butter and mix for a few seconds, just until evenly incorporated.

Fill individual silicone moulds about two-thirds full of the batter (or see the tip). Bake in the preheated oven for 15–18 minutes, until the edges are golden brown and a skewer inserted into the centre comes out clean. Allow to cool in the pan for 10 minutes, then remove to a wire rack to cool completely.

{*tip*}

If you don't have silicone financier moulds, you can use a silicone or a greased regular bun tin instead.

Treacle tart

Elaine Murphy, The Winding Stair

Home is any place where you feel safe and secure. It's a happy place, a sanctuary, somewhere to love and be loved, to create and flourish.

For me, this tart is the taste of Ireland. It brings a sense of the richness and culture that are synonymous with our streets and towns.

Serves 6–8

For the sweet pastry:

250g plain flour, sifted, plus extra for dusting

175g cold butter, diced, plus extra melted butter for greasing

75g icing sugar

2 egg yolks

1 tbsp cold water

For the filling:

150g day-old brown or white bread, crusts removed

650g golden syrup or 140g treacle

150g unsalted butter

1 egg

50ml double cream

zest of 2 lemons

a large pinch of salt

To serve:

clotted cream or ice cream

To make the pastry, put the sifted flour and butter in a large bowl and rub together using your fingertips until it resembles breadcrumbs. Add the icing sugar, egg yolks and water and mix until it comes together into a dough. Wrap in cling film, then chill in the fridge for 2 hours.

Grease a 23cm loose-bottomed tart case with melted butter, then dust it with flour, gently knocking out any excess. Line a baking tray with non-stick baking paper and put the prepared tart case on top.

Once the pastry has rested, roll it out on a lightly floured work surface until it's 4–5mm thick. Lift the rolled pastry into the prepared tart case, pressing it firmly into the case to mould it to the sides and bottom. Trim off any excess pastry, then chill in the fridge for 30 minutes.

Preheat the oven to 200°C (180°C fan).

Remove the tart case from the fridge and prick the base several times with a fork. Line the base and sides of the case with non-stick baking paper, then fill it with dried beans. Bake in the preheated oven for 30–35 minutes, until crisp and pale golden brown. Discard the paper and beans.

Meanwhile, to make the filling, blitz the bread in a food processor until it has formed breadcrumbs. Set aside.

Melt the golden syrup or treacle and the butter in a saucepan over a low to medium heat. Set aside to cool slightly.

In a large bowl, whisk together the egg and cream until well combined. Pour in the syrup and butter mixture and stir to combine, then stir in the breadcrumbs, lemon zest and a large pinch of salt until well combined.

Pour the filling into the cooked pastry case, then return the tart to the oven and bake for 40–45 minutes, until the filling is dark golden.

Allow the tart to cool slightly for 15 minutes before cutting into slices. Serve warm with clotted cream or ice cream.

Contributors

Ahmet Dede is a Turkish-born chef living in Ireland since 2009. After working in some of the best restaurants in Ireland and Europe, he opened his own restaurant, Dede at the Customs House, in 2020 and achieved a Michelin star within the first year. Ahmet's food is inspired by his heritage to create a Turkish fusion spice menu married with local West Cork produce. @ahmet_dede_

Aidan McGrath has worked for quite some time to promote and raise the standard of pub dining in Ireland, and his hard work and determination have not gone unnoticed. Aidan won a Michelin star for his robust, confident cooking in 2018 at Wild Honey Inn in County Clare, the first pub to be awarded a Michelin star for food in Ireland. @wildhoneyinn

Aishling Moore is one of Ireland's most exciting young chefs. Her fish restaurant, Goldie, in Cork has pioneered gill-to-fin cooking in Ireland while producing some of the best, most intriguing and dynamic modern Irish food. Sustainability is at the heart of her operation, where an 'all catch' approach ensures a good deal for local fishermen and a daily changing menu for guests. @aishlingmoore

Aisling and Michael Flanagan, a husband-and-wife team, make Velvet Cloud sheep's milk yogurt and cheese on their farm in Mayo, where Michael's family has been farming the land for generations. Velvet Cloud yogurt has nothing added and nothing strained away, just fresh sheep's milk and four live yogurt cultures. @velvetcloud.ie_

Anna Haugh began her career in her hometown of Dublin. In May 2019, she founded Myrtle Restaurant in Chelsea, London. Anna takes old Irish recipes and refines them, making the dishes more elegant but still with the heartbeat of Ireland. Anna has worked on numerous television shows for the BBC, is the resident chef on the *Morning Live* breakfast show and was a judge on *MasterChef: The Professionals*. @haughser

Anthony O'Toole specialises in turning business practices upside-down and making things happen. Anthony is also a gastronomy and craft activist, a chef and tutor, an accredited culinary professional and drinks sommelier, a biodiversity gardener, a cookbook collector and a writer on food, culture and travel. @anthonyotoole_

Aoife Noonan is an award-winning pastry chef who has worked in some of the best restaurants in Ireland. Aoife gives demos, patisserie masterclasses and online cooking classes, has worked as a culinary consultant and brand ambassador and wrote a weekly food column in the *Irish Times Magazine*. She recently moved to sunny Sydney, where she continues to develop her skills and pursue her love of all things sweet. @aoifenoonan_

Caitlin Ruth hails from Dublin, New Hampshire, USA, and has called Ireland her home since 1992. Formerly head chef of Deasy's restaurant near Clonakilty and listed in McKennas' 100 Best and awarded the Michelin Bib Gourmand, she now has a food truck, Caitlin Ruth Food, that serves a menu driven by seasonal food from West Cork's local growers and producers. @caitlinruthfood

Claire and Christopher Arnold are the brother-and-sister team behind Lennox Street Grocer in Dublin. Claire studied business and politics but ended up turning a passion for food into a career, first at the Dublin Cookery School, then at numerous restaurants in Ireland, France and Canada, then moving to front-of-house and discovering the world of wine. Christopher studied history and got his master's in advertising while making cocktails and tinctures in Dublin and Brooklyn and also working with Host restaurant for a few years as part of the front-of house team. @lennoxstreetgrocer

Danni Barry got a job washing pots in a local restaurant at 15 to start saving up for a car and fell in love with the atmosphere of a kitchen. She achieved a Michelin star for Deanes Eipic (2015–2017), becoming only the second female chef in Ireland to have received the accolade. Danni is currently the executive chef at Ballynahinch Castle. @danni_barry

Darina Allen is a well-known chef, author of 20 cookbooks and co-founder of the famous Ballymaloe Cookery School in the midst of a 100-acre organic farm in East Cork. Students come from all over the world to hone their culinary skills at this sustainable farm-to-table school established in 1983. @darina_allen

Denis Cotter is the owner and executive chef of Paradiso, the renowned vegetarian restaurant in Cork City, which he opened in 1993 and is built around a close working relationship with Gortnanain vegetable farm near the city. Paradiso remains at the forefront of innovative plant-based cooking. Denis is also the author of five cookbooks. @paradisocork

Domini Kemp is the author of five cookbooks and co-founder of the ITSA food group, overseeing multiple restaurants, cafés and event catering operations. She received her MA in Gastronomy and Food in

2019 and recently completed the Chartered Director Diploma in the IoD and a Pg Dip in Positive Health in the Royal College of Surgeons. She is studying for a Diploma in Culinary Medicine. @dominikemp

Dvir Nusery, who hails from Israel, is chef and co-owner of Mezze in Tramore, Waterford, which he runs with his Irish wife, Nicola Crowley. Together they share their take on recipes from Dvir's family, street food they enjoyed in Israel and inspiration from local produce. They love the concept of shared food experiences. @mezze.ie

Elaine Murphy has had a passion for food and hospitality ever since she was little, so she jumped at the chance to create a restaurant in The Winding Stair in 2006. The Winding Stair and its sister restaurants are all about local, Irish, simple, honest food. Elaine believes that taste, quality and excitement should be at the heart of everything we buy and serve. @thewindingstairdublin

Ellie Kisyombe spent many years working on the campaign to end direct provision. In 2015 she co-founded the OurTable social enterprise; in 2017 she trained at the Ballymaloe Cookery School; in 2019 she was the first asylum seeker to run for local election; and in 2021 she launched her range of vegan hot sauces inspired by her Malawian heritage, infused with the spices that remind her of home. @elliekisyombe

Eoin Cluskey, founder of Bread 41, believes that food is about bringing people together. At the heart of its ability to do that – and of the history of food – is real bread. Eoin is driven by a determination to better the future of the food industry and to create a food experience as authentic and unique as it is delicious. @bread41

Eva Pau grew up in the Asia Market store on Drury Street, Dublin, that is owned by her parents, Helen and Howard Pau. Asia Market celebrated its 40th anniversary in 2021 and is Ireland's largest Asian food importer, distributor and retailer, specialising in flavours and ingredients from all across Asia. @pau_pau_foods

Gareth Mullins has over 20 years' experience cooking in five-star hotels in Ireland and Australia. He was appointed executive chef at The Marker Hotel when it opened in Dublin in 2013 and is responsible for all menu design and food preparation in the hotel's four kitchens. Gareth makes frequent appearances on TV and radio, is a long-standing member of Euro-Toques Ireland and an advisory member of Chef Network. @garmullins

Gaz Smith is the mastermind behind Michael's, Big Mike's and Little Mike's, three restaurants in Dublin with a legion of loyal fans. He is also the co-author, along with Rick Higgins, of the award-winning cookbook *And for Mains: Stories, Recipes and Pints with an Irish Butcher and a Chef*. @michaels_dublin

Georgina Campbell was born on a small mixed farm in Cornwall, the foundation for a lifetime love of good, simple food. Georgina runs the independent Georgina Campbell's Ireland food and hospitality guides, is the author of several cookbooks and a founder member and current president of the Irish Food Writers' Guild. @irelandguide

Graham Herterich set up The Cupcake Bloke in 2012 and opened his retail store, The Bakery, in Rialto in 2018. Author of *Bake: Traditional Irish Baking with Modern Twists*, a Bosch ambassador and winner of several Blas na hÉireann Awards and Chef Ireland Awards, Graham creates tasty bakes with both conventional and unusual flavour combinations, using traditional Irish recipes as inspiration. @graham_herterich

Gráinne Mullins grew up in Galway with a love and respect for good food. After working in pastry in many of Ireland's leading kitchens, the self-taught chef was the winner of the prestigious 2019 Euro-Toques Young Chef of the Year. Channelling the skills, artistry and joy she has learned from some of the country's most talented chefs, Gráinne founded Grá Chocolates in 2020. @grainnemullins

Jack and Theo Kirwan are founders of Sprout & Co., a group of restaurants in Dublin serving local, seasonal and flavourful food, with a lot of the ingredients coming from their 40-acre organic farm just outside the city. The brothers have led the change in Dublin's fast food scene. 'Farm to fork' has never simply been a slogan for them – it is instrumental in their approach to food. @sproutandco

Jess Murphy is from New Zealand and has lived in Ireland since 2003. She opened her award-winning restaurant, Kai, with her Irish husband, Dave Murphy, in 2011. When Jess is not feeding or minding people, she is quietly fighting for an underdog somewhere here or abroad. She has been a formal High-Profile Supporter of the UNHCR since 2017. Everything that Jess does is based on friendship, relationships and respect. @kai_galway

Sally McKenna is a photographer, cookery editor, publisher of the McKennas' Guides and winner, with John, of the first ever André Simon Special Award. **John McKenna** has written about Ireland's food culture for 30 years and curates the annual *Sunday Times* 100 Best Restaurants in Ireland list. In 2018, Sally and John were each awarded an Honorary Fellowship by ATU Galway in recognition of their work describing Ireland's artisan food culture over three decades. @mckennasguides

Jp McMahon is a chef, restaurateur, author and culinary director of the EatGalway Restaurant Group, which comprises Cava Bodega and the Michelin-starred Aniar. Jp is committed to the educational and ethical aspects of food, to buying and supporting the best local and free-range produce, and to engaging directly with farmers and producers. Jp is also the founder and symposium director of Food on the Edge, one of the biggest international food events in Europe. @mistereatgalway

JR Ryall is the pastry chef at Ballymaloe House in County Cork. He has been working there since the age of 15 and in 2010 took the reins to oversee the dessert menu. Each year, he travels for two months in search of new culinary ideas around the world. He has also staged at The River Cafe, Ottolenghi, Chez Panisse and Tartine Bakery, among other esteemed restaurants. JR's debut cookbook, *Ballymaloe Desserts*, was published in 2022. @jrryall

Keith Coleman is co-founder of Roots, a roaming food project that works closely with small-scale growers and producers to bring unique dining experiences to interesting places. Keith's cooking journey began in earnest at the Fumbally Café and from there he has been involved in a myriad of interesting projects. Keith currently works as a caretaker and private chef on a country estate in Cavan. @keithjamescoleman

Kevin Burke found his calling at an early age and after studying Culinary Arts at DIT, he was offered a position at Restaurant Patrick Guilbaud, Ireland's only two-Michelin-star restaurant at the time, where he developed a passion for French cooking and an appreciation of the importance of high-quality produce. His culinary journey then took him to London but he returned to Dublin in 2019 and worked alongside the Allta team. Kevin opened Library Street in 2021. @kevinkbburke

Kristin Jensen is the publisher at Nine Bean Rows, Blasta Books and *Scoop* food magazine. Frustrated that many voices and many parts of Ireland's food culture were not being represented, she founded this boutique publishing house for tastemakers and storytellers in 2021 to update the story of the modern, diverse and vibrant food scene in Ireland. @edibleireland

Kwanghi Chan was born in Hong Kong and moved to Buncrana, Donegal, when he was eight years old. After training in his family's traditional Chinese restaurant and takeaway, he has gone on to work in Michelin-starred kitchens, his own street food truck and everything in between. He now runs his Bites by Kwanghi restaurants and ChanChan Asian Sauces. @kwanghic

Lily Ramirez-Foran – shopkeeper, author, storyteller, mad dreamer and lover of all things Irish – is the founder of Ireland's first Mexican boutique grocer and cookery school, Picado Mexican in Dublin. Lily has been living and cooking in Ireland for 20 years with her Irish husband and business partner, Alan. She's a woman on a mission to showcase Mexican food beyond its clichés and misconceptions. @lily_ramirezforan

Manuela Spinelli specialises in food projects and has extensive practical experience in event management in the culinary field in Ireland and abroad. She is Secretary-General of Euro-Toques Ireland, a community of chefs and cooks that works to preserve Irish culinary heritage and support traditional cooking methods while promoting producers of local and seasonal artisan products. She has also provided language support for some of the world's biggest events and businesses. @manuspins

Mark Anderson has 25 years of experience in Ireland and internationally working across all sectors of the hospitality industry. He joined Gather & Gather in 2015 as their first culinary director in Ireland. In that role he has pushed the boundaries of workplace catering for clients in various sectors, with health and taste to the fore. In recent years, Mark has also been a founding member of the National Advisory Council of Chef Network and a Food on the Edge ambassador and partner. @markybhoy70

Michelle Darmody is an activist, researcher and award-winning food writer whose writing brings together food, creativity and sustainability. Michelle is currently completing a PhD, focusing on food education for Irish primary school children. Her fieldwork projects have led to winning RETHINK Ireland Social Innovation funding for a nationwide Food and Biodiversity Programme as well as the Irish Food Writers' Guild Community Food Award.

Neven Maguire is chef-proprietor of the award-winning MacNean House and Restaurant in Blacklion, Cavan. He is well known for his TV programmes on RTÉ and regular radio contributions and has published many popular and award-winning cookbooks. @nevenmaguire

Niall Sabongi is a chef and restaurant owner turned seafood wholesaler. He created the Klaw group of restaurants for a more casual take on the finest seafood. Together with his wholesale business, Sustainable Seafood Ireland, Niall is on a mission to bring seafood to the people. @niallsabongi

Olivia Duff has a multifaceted role in Irish food: she is a hotelier, food and drink producer, programme director of Samhain Festival of Irish Food and Culture and regional leader in collaborative food tourism. As the founding creator of the Boyne Valley Food Series, Olivia has inspired other regions to tell their food story too and is working to create Ireland's first Centre of Food Culture. @gourmet_farmerette

Pat Whelan is the fifth generation of his family to be involved in farming and meat production and took over James Whelan Butchers from his parents in 1999. Pat is Ireland's first online butcher, a founding member of the Tipperary Food Producers Network and Great Taste Supreme Champion 2015. He has been recognised by Rick Stein as an Irish Food Hero and is the author of two cookbooks. @whelan_pat

Paula McIntyre is a chef, food writer and broadcaster. She has published three books, writes weekly columns in the *Newsletter* and

Belfast Telegraph, does a cooking slot on Radio Ulster's *John Toal Show* and is a regular panellist on Radio 4's *Kitchen Cabinet*. Her TV show, *Paula McIntyre's Hamely Kitchen*, was first shown in 2021. She is also the director of Slow Food Northern Ireland. @paulacooks

Peter Hannan is the only producer ever to win Supreme Champion of the Great Taste Awards twice and was a Golden Fork winner for five consecutive years. Hannan Meats supplies over 400 restaurants throughout Ireland, the UK and Europe and Peter has won a host of awards and accolades, including an MBE for Outstanding Contribution to Economic Development in Northern Ireland. @meatpeter

Richie Castillo is the chef behind Bahay, a Filipino pop-up restaurant that he runs with his partner, Alex O'Neill. Richie was born and raised in Dublin to an Irish mother and Filipino father. He spent 10 years working in various kitchens but after being put out of work during the pandemic, he decided to go out on his own and do his own thing. Richie and Alex named Bahay after the Tagalog word for home. @bahay_dub

Rick Higgins is a fourth-generation butcher. A dry age specialist, he mixes traditions with modern techniques, specially selecting and sourcing the meat from small farms across Ireland and dry ageing all their produce on the bone. A nose-to-tail butcher, Higgins Butchers is one of the last remaining true master butchers in Ireland. @higgins_butchers

Russell Alford and Patrick Hanlon are the pair behind GastroGays. The duo began their award-winning blog a decade ago and have amassed an international audience since then. They are also behind the successful food podcast Chew the Fat and the long-form food writing Substack newsletter, Chip Paper. Their debut cookbook, *Hot Fat*, was published in 2022. They are also the restaurant critics for *Sunday Times Ireland*. @gastrogays

Ruth Healy, proprietor of Urru Culinary Store in Bandon, is a second-generation Cork-based shopkeeper. Her experiences in Japan, London, blue-chip business, Ballymaloe Cookery School and Irish Food Culture studies have coalesced into making Urru an exemplar of Irish food retail. Ruth has co-founded food trails and farmers markets and was a Fáilte Ireland Irish Food Champion. @urrubandon

Ruth Hegarty is the director of egg&chicken consulting, an agency focused on food policy, food education and the development of diverse, sustainable food systems. Ruth has dedicated her career to advocating for small food producers and farmers; a fairer, cleaner food system; and access to good food for all. @eggandchick

Sally Barnes has run her award-winning fish-smoking business for more than 40 years. Now she is sharing her knowledge of the natural world and the wonders therein by teaching smoking and foraging skills to younger generations keen to know how we preserved available foods in times gone by before those skills vanish. @woodcocksmokery

Santosh Thomas and his wife, Milie Mathews, run 3 Leaves, the Michelin-recommended Indian restaurant in Blackrock, Dublin. They started as a tiny stall in Blackrock Market, preparing Indian food that was lovingly cooked and served with the warmest service and never-ending smiles. @3leavesblackrock

Siobhán Ní Ghairbhith, an ex-primary school teacher, has been leading her team at St Tola goat farm since 1999, bringing it from a small artisanal, seasonal business to an internationally recognised brand. Sustainability and honest food with true provenance are at the core of Siobhán's philosophy and her sense of place and its culture is true to all that she does. @st.tolaqueen

Sunil Ghai is the chef and restaurateur at the award-winning Pickle, Tiffin and Street Indian restaurants. After discovering new tastes, new relationships and histories in the food of countries he has travelled and lived in and rediscovering those from his own upbringing in India, Sunil is recreating, reimagining and renewing those culinary memories for his family, friends and customers. @pickle_bysunil

Suzanne Campbell writes on food and farming issues for Irish newspapers as well as reporting for RTÉ radio and television. She is a former series producer of the RTÉ television series *Ear to the Ground* and has won the International Farming Journalist of the Year broadcast award. She is the co-author of the book *Basketcase* and has written two documentaries on food for RTÉ television. She also runs the Irish Food Writing Awards. @campbellsuz

Tara Gartlan is a pastry chef who has worked in some of Ireland's most prestigious restaurants, where precision, dedication and artistry are at the forefront. While studying Culinary Arts in DIT Cathal Brugha Street, focusing on pastry and nutrition, Tara was diagnosed with coeliac disease, which pushed her to further her knowledge of and interest in gluten-free baking and patisserie. @taragartlan

Tara Walker was the owner and chef tutor at the East Coast Cookery School in Termonfeckin, Louth for 13 years and is the author of the book *Good Food No Stress*. She grew up in a family of food businesses and honed her profession at Le Cordon Bleu, Paris. Tara appears regularly on Virgin Media One's *Ireland AM* and has a monthly cookery slot on the LMFM radio station. @tarawalkerchef

Wade Murphy has worked in top kitchens in London, Europe and the US as well in Ireland. He opened 1826 Adare in 2013, which he owns with his wife, Elaine. 1826 Adare was awarded a Bib Gourmand from the *Michelin Guide to Great Britain and Ireland*, which Wade considers to be one of the highlights of his career to date. @chefwademurphy

Index

Acknowledgements

Across the country, millions of us take it for granted that we finish the day enjoying a meal in the sanctuary of our homes. But this is only the reality for some.

At Gather & Gather, our ethos is all about using food to bring people together to enjoy good conversation and great company, whatever the time or place. Food is our world; it's what we know best. So in 2019, having decided to work on a fundraising project that would support the efforts of the Peter Mc Verry Trust, it made sense that we would bring together our well-established food community to help us succeed.

Our ambition was to create a cookbook filled with recipes from food lovers around Ireland that would reflect their memories of home while also raising awareness around homelessness and the outstanding work of the Peter McVerry Trust.

We reached out to Ireland's bakers, butchers, farmers, food champions, producers, shopkeepers and chefs to get involved with our cookbook project, with all proceeds going to the Trust. And oh boy, did we get a response! Thank you to everyone for their offers of help and support. It feels good to be in a position to acknowledge the fantastic people who jumped in on this journey and the contributions they have made to this beautiful book.

To Mark Anderson, our culinary director, who took the lead on this project and faced the challenge with great determination, using his persuasive skills to coax people into supporting our idea along the journey to getting it into print. A special mention to our MD, Pauline Cox, for saying 100% yes to the initial idea; to the creative input from Federica Mann, Victoria Navas and Laura Middleton, who have advised, supported and encouraged this project from day one; and to Diarmuid Doyle for all his help in fundraising.

A very special thank you to Pat Doyle, CEO of Peter McVerry Trust, who exemplifies the fantastic work of the Trust in allowing us to help in a way that offers hope and respect.

A shout-out goes to William Tallon for making the first introduction to the Peter McVerry Trust and provoking us into thinking about how we could do something to help.

And of course thank you to the stars of the show, our contributors. Without them sharing their cherished recipes, we wouldn't have gathered this beautiful collection together. Volunteering their recipes is akin to giving back to their community; we thank them all for doing that. There's something here for everyone and for every occasion. We hope you love these recipes as much as we do.

Bringing this all to life has been the selfless work of Kristin Jensen of Nine Bean Rows, who, along with designer Jane Matthews and photographer Katie Quinn, helped us to pull an idea and a dream together into what we feel is a very special book.

To all the wonderful Peter McVerry Trust volunteers and teams at this fantastic charity who do amazing work providing a route off the streets and into safety.

And finally, thank you to this book's sponsors,
who all donated so graciously because we asked for their help:

All Type	Hugh Jordan	Musgrave	Sisu
Broderick Bros	Java	Ready Chef	Stafford Lynch
Caterwaiter	Kish	Robinson Meats	Unilever
Excel Recruitment	La Rousse	Select Hire	Wholefoods

NINE
BEAN
ROWS

Nine Bean Rows

23 Mountjoy Square

Dublin

D01 E0F8

Ireland

@9beanrowsbooks

ninebeanrowsbooks.com

First published 2023

© Gather & Gather Ireland, 2023

ISBN: 978-1-9993799-9-5

General editor: Kristin Jensen

Design and layout: Jane Matthews janematthewsdesign.com

Food photography and styling: Katie Quinn katiequinnphotography.net

Home economist: Susan Papazian

Printed by L&C Printing Group, Poland

The paper in this book is produced using pulp from managed forests.